BURY MY HEART AT CHUCK E. CHEESE'S

Tiffany Midge

Foreword by Geary Hobson

University of Nebraska Press | Lincoln

Library of Congress
Control Number: 2019005854

Designed and set in Arno Pro by L. Auten.

For all my badass grandmas

Gag me with a coup stick.

—NDN Valley Girl

Me: *How do you say pseudo-intellectual in Lakota?*
Sherwin B.: *Siouxdo intellectual.*

—exchange on Facebook

Contents

Foreword

Geary Hobson

Over time (too much time, if you ask me) Native American people have generally been portrayed by the dominant culture as being entirely without the least vestiges of humor. Stolid, dour, ready to pounce on you (if you are white) and take away that unnecessary scalp. (And of course, if you are Louis L'Amour, that's all that Indians do!) Too much James Fenimore Cooper, Robert Montgomery Bird, William Gilmore Simms, Henry Wadsworth Longfellow, nearly every Puritan scribbler that ever was—even Mark Twain (the premier funny man of American letters himself), Hemingway, Faulkner—and, oh, the list can go on. For them Indians are without the least flicker of a smile, a half-joke or two, a grin, not a tickle in the ribs, nothing. Despite such nearly ignored portrayals by Washington Irving in *A Tour on the Prairies*, in which at one point he describes some Osage warriors around a campfire, laughing and joking and doing drumbeats with fists on their chests, cracking up Irving and his fellow tourists with their antics—this in 1832. Yes, non-Indian American people, humor does exist among Native American people. And much more present than the average reader probably seems likely to imagine.

But it has always been there, in the writing as well as the living. Washington Irving wasn't wrong. Just a glance at the writings by certain Native writers will effectively bear this out. Take the nineteenth century, the Century of Dishonor, when Natives were beginning to adapt to the reading and writing of the dominant culture in which they were being forced to become a part—you will find humor and often quite surprising at most times. Just as the post–Civil War era knew the writings of American funny guy journalists such as Twain himself and Josh Billings, Peter Finlay Dunne (Mr. Dooley and Company), and others, there was a similar rise of Native American journalists as well in tribal newspapers of the day. DeWitt Duncan Clinton, Alexander L. Posey (Fus Fixico), Joseph Lynch (Uncle Joe) Martin, Woochee Oochee, Dan Madrano (for more on this, just check out the now-classic work by Daniel F. Littlefield Jr. and James W. Parins, *A Bio-Bibliography of Native American Writing, 1772–1924*). All this "funny Indian stuff" was actually made international in scope and outlook by someone who carried the humor of Indians to surprising heights and locales—the Cherokee writer, cowboy, and movie star Will Rogers. Some say, "He's a funny guy because he's mostly white." No, gentle reader, examine Rogers's humor more closely, and you will find that it is very much a product of the milieu he came from: relocated Indians doing their best to survive in the dominant culture into which they were dumped.

And Indian humor continues to the present day and, I strongly believe, grows more potent and deadly with each generation. Here are a few to scan for a laugh or two from the first wave of the Native American literary renaissance (1968–92): the Airplane Man segment of James Welch's now classic *Winter in the Blood*. There's Simon Ortiz's personal expressions and reactions attendant on the birth of his and the renowned poet Joy Harjo's daughter—Rainy Dawn—as he awaited Rainy's coming into the world, in "Notes for My Child," in which, though anxious and apprehensive, he records his experience with wonderful humor and humanity. And how about the work of Gerald Vizenor, Carter Revard, Jim Northup, LeAnne Howe—here, without equivocation, you will find mucho laughs amid scenes of deep seriousness. And then, in the second phase of the Renaissance (1992 to the present), there's the hilarious plot line of D. L. Birchfield's short story "Never Again," in which a Choctaw brother persuades his sibling to accompany him on a long, several days hiking and camping expedition in the Ouachita Mountains, without telling the younger brother that a severe snowstorm is expected in the region and then gets a kick out of the whole thing when the younger brother is totally unprepared by wearing summerlike clothing and using a thin sleeping bag. And also by Donny Birchfield, how about the titles of two of his books: *How Choctaws Invented Civilization and How Choctaws Will Conquer the World* and *The Oklahoma Basic Intelligence Test*? Indeed, they say it all, with just about a laugh on every page. And how about Diane Burns's "Sure You Can Ask Me a Personal Question," in which the poet lampoons certain non-Indians' often dim-wittedness about the most basic things regarding Indians, such as why do they have black hair and high cheekbones? And of course, there's Drew Hayden Taylor and his *Funny, You Don't Look like One* (with three sequels) and *Only Drunks and Children Tell the Truth* as well as all the funny stuff to be found in the writings of Craig S. Womack, Tim Tingle, William S. Yellow Robe Jr., Richard Van Camp, Dawn Dumont, and Kateri Akiwenzie-Damm—all, more often than not, as funny as a rubber crutch.

And now Tiffany Midge, and particularly the book at hand— heck, the title alone is guaranteed to crack you up. Whoever heard or even thought of Chuck E. Cheese's with regard to Native American literature? (Where are our bison and war paint and tomahawks and "ughs" and "Hows"?) Good grief, dear reader, what are we up against? This Midge lady comes along and dumps one little story or vignette after another, all guaranteed to funny you up like wildfire. Just as I mentioned about Birchfield and Company, look at a few of Ms. Midge's titles—"How Sacagawea Got Her Groove Back," "The Wild West (Wing) and Wild Bill Hiccup," "Hey, America, I'm Taking Back Thanksgiving," "Ghoul,

Interrupted," and of course, the book's title—now I ask you, ain't these all belly whoppers?

Here's a selection of a few of the one-liners (laughing out loud is permitted):

"Being that so many white people believe that Indians practice magic, you'd think they'd try and be nicer to us."

"For a thousand dollars I'll teach you Native American rituals. The first cleansing rite involves you, a brush, ammonia, and my kitchen floor."

"As a Native American wordsmith, I use *every* part of the sacred sentence."

"All this talk about the depth and richness of his skin made me think she wanted to make a skin suit from his hide."

"I will fight no more about putting the toothpaste cap back on the tube forever."

"Vice President Pence with a Myspace page, "MikeyLikesIt.""

Thanks to Tiffany Midge, I'm anxiously awaiting, hopefully, the next time I click on my TV, the latest episode of Melania Trump's new show, *The Billionaire and the Showgirl*, in which a segment entitled "Ted Nugent and Duck Dynasty for a Roadside Brunch" is aired.

And now, here's my favorite: "Trump Pardons Zombie Apocalypse," in which zombies, having "wreaked havoc in the streets by attacking and eating peoples' brains" and then being imprisoned during the Obama administration, are pardoned by The Donald—keeping to his promise to undo all the damage done by the previous president. Trump Tweets that the zombies "were just doing their job."

So now, you want you a laugh or two? Then go find you an Indian seems to be the message here. But like I been saying all along, we sho-nuff got some right here—all guaranteed to tickle your funny bone in more ways than jist a (s)midge.

BURY MY HEART AT CHUCK E. CHEESE'S

I

My Origin Story
Is a Cross between
"Call Me Ishmael,"
a Few Too Many
Whiskey Sours
Packed in an Old Thermos
at the Drive-In Double
Feature, and That Little
Voice That Says,
"You Got This"

Bury My Heart at Chuck E. Cheese's

The day of my mother's funeral service, I separated myself from the rest of the grieving throng and hid out in the musician's belfry like tortured Quasimodo, my grief too hideous to expose.

I peered down upon the mourners below, watched my aunts struggling with folding a star quilt, trying to contain it within the casket. The lid wouldn't close. The white pastor believed my mother's quilt was some sort of ancient Lakota ritual. He announced it with gravity and a sense of suspicious distance.

Native flute music floated out from the speakers as my aunties struggled to close the lid, both furtively cramming the ends of the quilt into the casket, tucking my mother inside. One of them gestured exasperatingly to the other, and then they both started to laugh.

*

Months before her death, my mother made me promise that we'd bury her in her royal-blue pantsuit, her favorite color. She forced her jewelry on me—take this and this . . . here, take this . . .

It is both touching and morbid to accept a dying woman's most personal belongings: her favorite silver and turquoise earrings, the onyx bracelet, the Black Hills gold rings.

She even gave me her little silver buffalo pendant. I wore it to a grade school presentation, and one of the children raised her hand and asked, "Is that a pig?"

*

The crucial difference between having children versus having pets is that when your sister's cat gets run over by a car, you can say things like "She never was very bright."

*

"Wakes lasted for days," my mother says. "We'd get bored waiting around while the old people sat huddled over like crows. Sometimes we'd tell the younger kids that the hosts needed to use the outhouse for extra storage until it was time for the deceased to be buried. We'd tell the kids that it was a multiple fatality car accident, lots of parts that needed storing. Those kids refused to use the outhouse after that."

*

On the day my mother received her test results, we stopped off at a restaurant for lunch. The waitress complimented my mother on her earrings. My mother laughed. "You want them? I won't be needing them."

*

Grandma Iron Thunder's service was held on a scorching day in the middle of August on the Dakota plains. There was gold-colored grass and blinding sky for miles in every direction. Her casket was draped with a red quilt featuring the famous silhouette *The End of the Trail* stitched in black cloth. My mother clucked, "I hate that quilt—good thing they're burying it."

*

Following the fire and brimstone of my mother's memorial service, I wended my way down the spiral staircase from the musician's belfry, and a church lady I'd never met before congratulated me on my beautiful singing. "You have such a beautiful voice!" she cooed. I thanked her, taking the credit, even though I had not been singing at all.

*

On November 22, 1963, at the doctor's office, my mother and her husband received news that he had six months to live. Immediately following the short walk to their car, Frank switched on the radio, and they listened briefly to the story about the assassination of President Kennedy. Then they switched off the radio and started driving back home to spend time with their new baby daughter.

*

My Grandma Wing's funeral was held in the old church and cemetery at Fort Peck. She requested everyone wear white. She was ninety-eight. The service was dignified and affecting, replete with a mix of traditional and Christian songs. As the service was finishing up and people were paying their respects, a melee erupted outside. A dozen or more cousins jumped Rachel's baby daddy and beat him to a pulp. All those white shirts and all those white pants stained with blood and dirt. Someone said, "Clyde's Last Stand." The men all laughed.

*

During a trip to Mexico, my sister tattooed my mother's name, Alita Rose, surrounded by roses onto her ankle. A few years later, following the death of my father, I considered getting a tattoo in tribute to him also, but Herman Lloyd just didn't have the same cachet.

*

When my mother's respirator was finally removed and we watched the monitors slowly wind down . . . and when I finally left the hospital, a three-year girl refused to let me pass her until I acknowledged her ecstatic announcement: *We. Just. Had. A. Baby.*

5

*

The Lakota unburdened themselves of hair, of fingers, cut into their flesh to temporarily escape the grief of a loved one's death. I saw this on *A Man Called Horse* and in *Dances with Wolves*. But as far as I knew, no one in my immediate family had ever done this. My mother was worth far more than a hank of hair. She was worth my spine. My eyes. My womb.

*

There are many versions of the scenes that take place inside my head—a dying mother instructs her daughter with her last wishes—but the one I remember the most is poached from a meme making the rounds online . . .

"I want my remains spread at Disneyland," my mother says. "But I don't want to be cremated. Just leave my parts."

"Okay. I promise."

"You can bury my heart at Chuck E. Cheese's."

"Okay. You got it."

"Bury my heart at Sea World."

"I will, Mama."

"I will fight no more about putting the toothpaste cap on, forever."

We were two Indian women, laughing until our bellies ached, spitting death right in the eye.

Headlines

I've been saving newspaper clippings, curious human interest stories to inspire my writing efforts. A cache of yellowed newsprint lies in a small pile:

Woman charged with death of overfed toddler

Man married twenty-nine times will have funeral

Mermaid girl to have legs split

One clipping is particularly compelling: *Mother's coma ends after sixteen years.* The woman resurrected from her coma is Standing Rock Sioux. She emerged from her sixteen-year sleep on Christmas Eve, and her nickname is Happy, which makes me think of *The Seven Dwarfs*, which makes me think of another Disney icon, Sleeping Beauty, a more apt attribution.

My headlines collection today is harvested mostly from Facebook newsfeeds:

The day my pastor claimed gay people are possessed
by fart demons that can drive pigs to suicide

Charles Manson's wedding canceled—
bride "just wanted his corpse" to make money

Idaho lawmaker wonders if women could
have gyno exam by swallowing a little camera

Years ago I watched a TV movie starring Elizabeth Montgomery from *Bewitched.* The movie was about a woman who reemerged

7

after being in a coma for over a decade. Her readjustment from having been a popular high school cheerleader to being poised on the edge of middle age met with harrowing challenges. A handsome high school basketball coach fell in love with her and aggressively pursued her, trying to break down the barriers of her "teenage" shyness, which culminated in the literal breaking down of her door yelling, "Love me!" She finally submitted. These days there'd be a twelve-step group for what the basketball coach was afflicted with, not to mention a restraining order.

Pastor claims women are penis homes
and men's penises belong to God

My aunt Carlotta suffered a brain aneurysm and never woke up. She'd always been active and in good health. She and her husband had just adopted a little boy; she sent us pictures. And then abruptly—silence. For nearly two decades she slept, wasted away, slept, growing thinner and thinner, sleeping and sleeping, in a convalescent home outside Glasgow, Montana. Her husband remarried. Her little boy grew up and married. Relatives passed away. Presidents served out their terms, were reelected, served out those terms. More headlines: the Berlin wall fell. The United Nations declared war in the Middle East. Waco. O. J. Simpson. Oklahoma City terrorism. Cloned sheep. First black president. My aunt slept. And slept.

Practical help for the demon possessed: Vatican rolls out
new exorcism course

Some thought my aunt was the victim of Indian witchery. A jealous enemy perhaps. An imagined trespass or a real trespass. I don't know that I believe in those things. I don't know if I even believe in ghosts. Believing might only allow such things to surface. Once I wished out loud for a woman to be dead, and the next year she died, her body blooming with tumors. She was my boyfriend's old lover, a kindled old flame, and was a catalyst for the breakup of his marriage, a wedge in his relationships that followed. Like with me. I was not the only woman in his life who seethed with jealousy.

Woman in sumo wrestler suit assaults ex-girlfriend in gay pub after she waved at man dressed as Snickers bar

My father had dated Aunt Carlotta before he met and married my mother. Carlotta was my mother's sister-in-law. It was less than a year after my mother's husband died that my mother married my father—her sister-in-law's ex-lover. I wish I knew why my dad and Carlotta broke up. I don't know if there was any animosity between my mother and Carlotta; they always seemed to be good friends. But you never know. It is easy to become confused about these things.

Students cook and serve grandparents

My mother's best friend in Havre, Montana, Twila, was stricken with a troubled marriage. Maybe *stricken* is the wrong word; it wasn't like getting the flu, but then again, maybe a troubled marriage *is* like getting the flu. If I can wish someone dead, certainly someone else could catch a bad marriage, that marital virus that's going around, maybe even a hex. Twila's husband stalked her whenever she went out. He thought she was running around on him. Mason stowed away in the trunk of her Riviera, and she caught him when she put groceries in the trunk. On another night my mother dropped by to visit, and as she was getting out of her car to walk up to the house, she discovered Mason perched twelve feet high in the branches of a tree, spying on his wife.

Man with nothing to declare has fifty-five tortoises in his pants

The Lakota word for *horse* is *sunka wakan*: *wakan*, which translates to "sacred" or "mystery" and *sunka*, meaning "dog." The Sioux are a horse culture, and the horse is highly revered, a spiritual being. This makes my childhood allergies to horsehair particularly ironic. It would have been hard for me if I lived in olden times. I was also allergic to rabbit fur as a child. This seems less of a problem, since as far as I know rabbits aren't especially revered. Not like horses, anyway. I suppose my father didn't take this into account—the fact that my mother was Lakota and raised on a reservation in eastern Montana—when he brought home what looked like a gift and presented it to my mother. It was a package wrapped in brown butcher paper and tied off with white string. Words were exchanged between my parents, voices raised, some alarm, and then my mother rushed from the kitchen in tears. My father calmly pulled out a fry pan, unwrapping the meat from its brown paper and cooking it like it was any other.

*PETA suggests Washington Redskins keep
controversial name, change logo to potato*

I learned of death's paradoxes when I was six—how acts of violence are sometimes demonstrations of mercy, even love. Along a Pacific beach he found a wounded mallard and applied an ax to end its suffering. From flight and prey to a naturalist's specimen, the mallard submitted to an inexact science—one of air and wind, one of pressure and temperature, one of sand and ocean salt. Among the viscera and ruins my father indicated the transparent bubble—*this is how it floats*. A fretwork of shadow and light, the blood mirrored the portentous reading of clouds, a swirl of lines and curves from where a song begins.

Emotional support pig kicked off flight for being disruptive

The last time I ever saw Jeff alive, he gave me a gift—an hour-glass. And it took over two decades later for the symbolism to finally dawn on me: an hourglass, gifted from a young man with one foot planted in the next world. His time was running out. Even the hourglass he gifted me appeared to have been stolen—I imagine from the desktop of one of the school classrooms he was hired to clean. Not borrowed time but stolen.

Old man, ninety-eight, wins lottery, dies next day

Agoraphobic grandma finally leaves home, immediately falls down manhole

"When were these photos taken?" I ask my mother. We are removing items from her dresser drawers, taking inventory to prepare for the day she will die. She has lung cancer. I hold up the black-and-white photos for her to see. I have never seen them before. There are three pictures, all taken in the same location, some isolated forest road. She looks gorgeous, disheveled, dreamy. They are from an earlier era, the seventies, taken when I was still very small, when I lived with both of my parents, my sister, and my grandfather. The photos were taken by her lover, a man my mother admits was a close friend of our family. I barely remember him. She hid the pictures away for years.

The Eagle *has landed, two men walk on the moon*

Chronicles of an affair with his secretary, found in an abandoned suitcase

Lana Turner's daughter fatally stabs her mother's lover

II

Instead of a
"Raised by
Wolves"
T-Shirt, Mine
Says "Raised by
Functional
Alcoholics
with
Intimacy
Phobias &
Low Self-
Esteem"

The Jimmy Report

Thursday, May 7, 2004, 11:00 a.m., Bellingham, WA

I pass by the front counter and spot him in the back climbing out from beneath a massive pile of textiles. He's wearing dark-blue polyester pants from a deceased World War II veteran's closet. The pants have multicolored dashes woven into the fabric that look like a moth infestation. They're obviously too big for him, and he belts them with an orange scarf.

Jimmy owns and operates Blue Moon Vintage Clothing, housed in a proverbial bulwark near the waterfront in the old-town section of Bellingham. I happen to catch him on a good day. His mood's up due to a windfall—the aforementioned massive pile of used clothes—from a guy he knows in the wholesale business, some kind of rag dealer. The clothes seem okay, usable, but looks can be deceiving.

I mentally list the pile's contents. A black bustier in a child's size 2M; a wispy blouse that appears at first glance to be leopard print but is actually owls; Ziggy Stardust shoes; acid-green poly-plaid golf pants (real beauts, Jimmy says, but too small for him) and a matching green Nebraska Tech College T-shirt; a purse with tags still attached; a red faux-leather trench coat à la Audrey Hepburn; tennis shirts from the Bruce Jenner Collection; assorted western-style shirts, the snappy kind.

Jimmy chirps about how he *isn't* selling his business after all, the pile of new clothes apparently the culprit for his optimism. Not to be a naysayer, but I'm not sure there is a thousand dollars' worth of merchandise in his pile, even with the fetching owl print blouse. Obviously, it makes him happy to think so, things looking up from his previous month's "donation" to the local Lummi tribe—aka the casino's craps table—so who am I to rain on his parade? While I'm relieved he isn't bailing out this week, next week could be different. Eventually, the property management is going to want its back rent, money that Jimmy professes not to have.

Jimmy relays that Paris Texas, the store next door, had been sniffing around his property the month before and that he's contemptuous of their hipster posturing and their empty brand of style. He thinks they pander to a faux counterculture, a type of trust fund street waif, which offends his sensibilities because Jimmy considers himself to be the genuine article. His clients don't pose as poverty-stricken, homeless addicts and alcoholics; they *are* poverty-stricken, homeless addicts and alcoholics. Many are Mission residents or railroad car buddies, apparently. I want to say mostly men who are down on their luck and who possess hearts of gold, but that'd be a cliché. A pair of Alaskan Natives appear on the sidewalk in front of the store, and Jimmy rushes out to greet them, slapping one guy on the back and mumbling something about stolen lands and Custer. The pair and others drop by the store frequently throughout the day because Jimmy gives them cigarettes, and all that's required in return is that they stand still long enough for Jimmy to tell them a funny story.

For me Jimmy's the quintessential everyman's man, champion of the underdog. I admire his contempt for capitalism and corporate sellouts. Part of what drives his decision not to sell his store is that his retail neighbor wants the space to expand, and he delights in denying them what they want, as if he's staying afloat simply out of spite. (As he once said, "If someone told me I couldn't be a Roman Catholic priest, I would be!") He posted a sign in the window of Blue Moon—written on the back of a poster for *Beat Angel*, an independent film he starred in—that conveyed his disdain and informed his patrons that the rumors weren't true: "Not Selling Out to Paris Texas!"

Scanning the expanse of the store, I ask him where his Goth girl clerks are, and Jimmy says they're probably tired of being paid in only clothes, adding that his employees are the only reason he's able to stay afloat because, unlike him, they aren't constantly wheeling and dealing and slashing prices on a whim. He regularly greets his customers with a rousing "Everything's half off! More if it looks good on you!" He's excellent with his regular customers: they'll wander in, and he directs them to their preferences and sizes—like a good bartender who always remembers the customers' usual. A man and woman come in and ask whether Jimmy has any leather chaps. The man is unusually tall, and the woman is unusually short. Some days the Blue Moon looks like the set of a Fellini picture. Jimmy pushes a cart of clothes free for the taking out to the sidewalk. He boasts that Bellingham has the best-dressed homeless in the country, largely due to him.

Friday, May 8, 2004, 8:00 9:30 a.m., Bellingham, WA
I visited Jimmy the day before to confirm our plans for a hunting and gathering errand to Skagit Valley thrift shops. The ironic T-shirt and trucker caps department is running critically low, and he's out of vintage slips. We made plans to restock. He doesn't have a car or a license, so I offered to help him out. Jimmy complains, "No one dresses up anymore." He's referring to the eighties, the thrift store glory days of Bananarama and Cyndi Lauper, that magical decade when New Wave celebrants and holdovers from the UK punk scene dressed up like serial killers or Ringling Bros. Circus clowns, the times before irony ruled supreme.

Jimmy phones at eight to set our meeting back to nine thirty, something about a gutter man. Good title for a book: "Waiting for the Gutter Man." I don't ask. When I get to the store to pick him up, Jimmy's sitting on the curb studying his shoes and gripping a brown paper sack filled with not alcohol but a collection of his personal effects: money, checks, ID, comb, etc. He blows into my car like a cyclone hitting a cattle barn.

As the car sits idling in the drive-in bank, I worry that we look like rookies in a drug cartel. A couple of ill-prepared, clumsy mules. The passenger floor is littered with checks and twenty-dollar bills, loose cigarettes, and change. Jimmy loses the pen; he can't manage to sign his name legibly, can't find his ID —it's a hot mess. Then he insists we visit McDonald's for breakfast, which delights him because he apparently doesn't have access to fast food restaurants living downtown and is excited about asking the drive-thru window guy if fellatio comes with the Happy Meal—or rather, the Happy Ending Meal, as he's decided to call it. We make a quick stop at the grocery store, where Jimmy buys a can of Crisco. I can't imagine why anyone would want to buy a giant can of Crisco at 10:00 a.m., but again, it's better not to ask. In addition to the Crisco, he feeds dollar bills into the scratch ticket machines and buys a seven-dollar lighter shaped like a rocket that shoots out sparks.

Our first stop is a retirement home thrift store somewhere near Stanwood. It's dollar bag day, and Jimmy, self-assured and in his element, gives off a heady note of swagger. What's better than Norwegian geriatrics and the musty clothes of the recently deceased? Each item has a story to tell, and we're intent upon keeping a running commentary. (1) The needlepoint kit resembling a flattened possum: "Nothing says Home Sweet Home better than a framed cross-stitch of roadkill." (2) The ribbon–and–plastic flora bound books: "An anti-literature craft project for wayward readers."

(3) The Costco-sized bottle of lotion, which was too expensive and put back on the shelf: "There goes your social life, Jimmy."

After stocking up on several grocery sacks of items, Jimmy narrowly escapes a physical altercation with Gladys, the volunteer clerk wearing a canary-yellow sundress. From what I manage to piece together, the proprietors are upset about Jimmy's lack of attention to tidiness. Apparently, on a previous visit Jimmy abandoned clothing items all over the aisles, on the floor, left them stranded on chairs, and forgot his baskets of items beneath the racks. Gladys isn't having any of it.

"Yeah, but I bought like nine bags of clothes." Jimmy insists. Nine dollars, I'm sure they really appreciated his business. Gladys remains unimpressed. And to be honest, I don't blame her one bit. Jimmy is the manifest version of the *Peanuts* character Pigpen, but instead of a cloud of dirt and debris, a cyclone swirls behind Jimmy's path, along with old beat-up trucks, cows, rusty wire mattresses, and road signs. I'm relieved we managed to get away before Jimmy made any further fuss or before Gladys called the cops.

Next stop: Camano Island for another dollar bag sale. That Jimmy, he's really got a bead on the secondhand goods! As we pull into the parking lot, we're greeted by a jaundiced man with a silver hook for a hand. A hook! Inside the store Jimmy really works up a froth; he tells the proprietors that he's picking up clothes for charities, like Evergreen Youth Home—at one point I overhear him telling a clerk that he's a priest and is picking up clothes for orphans at Paulie Shore's House of Casserole, which the clerk assumes is some kind of all-you-can-eat buffet. We cram more grocery bags into the trunk of my car. I gingerly suggest that he might consider holding off on shorts and tank tops and concentrate on adding to his winter-fall departments—a problem since

Jimmy seems mostly interested in buying trucker caps, T-shirts, and polyester men's suits. Stuff *he* wears.

Jimmy naps most of the way home. When he does manage to stay awake, he finishes his McDonald's sandwiches, tries reading part of a brochure on Northwest salmon out loud in a variety of celebrity impersonations, smokes a couple of cigarettes, and in his customary Jimmy style holds forth on a critique of Western civilization and his growing up in Queens as an Irish Catholic altar boy. He regales me with names and descriptions of all his homeless buddies, his married girlfriends, his epic drinking binges once upon a time on the Blackfeet Rez, and tells me about his partner in poetic crime sprees, the Lakota poet Luke Warm Water. Then he falls back asleep and a few minutes later awakens with a startled "Hey, baby!" When I pull up to the curb in front of Jimmy's store, I take an inventory of the inside of my car, which resembles the nest of a very large and messy bird—strewn newspapers, pamphlets, receipts, spilled bag of chips, crumbs in every crevice, cigarette ashes, scratch tickets, leftover McDonald's bags, used Kleenex, and the Safeway card Jimmy claims is his only form of ID.

I first met Jimmy at an independent film festival in Burbank. Jimmy played a spoken word poet in the aforementioned *Beat Angel*, an independent film about Jack Kerouac coming back from the dead. In it Kerouac's spirit lands in the body of a hobo bumming for change during a poetry open mic being held to celebrate Kerouac's birthday. The filmmaker was from Bellingham, as were many of the actors and crew. Jimmy's role was brief, just a flash compared to the rest of the film—he played the open mic's MC. But I must have watched and rewatched his scene dozens of times on video. He was so charismatic and interesting. He wore a Mad Men–style light-colored suit and a matching fedora. He was smoking a cigarette as he recited one of his original poems—I don't remember which one. It could have been from one of his chapbooks—*It Takes a Whole Mall to Raise a Child* or *Women Are from Venus, Men Are from Bars.* On the back covers of his chapbooks, more established poets wrote glowing reviews of Jimmy's work, saying he wrote in the tradition of Jack Kerouac or Charles Bukowski. One of his bios described him as having worked as a bouncer on the Blackfeet Indian Rez, as a welfare cheat, and as a plasma donor.

In Burbank during the film festival and within just a couple of hours of meeting him, he barged into my hotel room with all the grace of a jacked-up billy goat, jumped excitedly from topic to topic, picked up and handled most of my books and personal items, asked dozens of questions, paced from room to room, even checked out my closet—"Nice robe, I could sell these"—before scrambling out the door as if he was making a critical run for a toilet. That was his style. Hypermania. And it often left me feeling ramped up and exhilarated, like some kind of electrical storm had just touched down.

After *Beat Angel* premiered at one of the cinemas in Burbank, a group of us drove around, stopping off at different bars and small clubs. Outside one of the clubs, Jimmy introduced himself to a potpourri of hipsters smoking outside. He made the rounds, shaking everyone's hand, saying: "I'm Jimmy Henry. I'm a janitor at Hollywood High. I live in my parent's basement, and I collect gay bondage porn." And then later, at another restaurant, he offered to buy my friend and I a drink. But he didn't have any money, so he told us he'd be right back, then left us sitting at the table while he went outside to busk for spare change by reciting poetry on the street.

Sunday, April 11, 2004, 10:00 a.m., Bellingham, WA
I've been home a week after getting back from Burbank, and I happen to be hanging out at Stuart's, the coffee shop just around

the corner from Jimmy's store. I'm sitting in the upstairs balcony at Stuart's when I notice movement coming from the area across the length of tables at the wall opposite me. I look up from my book and watch in astonishment as a rather large section of the wall is being removed from the inside, then thumps to the floor. Next, a tall man in polyester plaid pants scuttles rodent-like through the hole and steps casually into the coffee shop, brushing himself off in a resolute kind of way before he turns back to the wall section, hoists it up, and fits it back into the wall like a piece of a life-sized jigsaw puzzle.

It's Jimmy. He has his own secret entrance from his apartment above the Blue Moon onto the balcony of Stuart's. When he notices me sitting at the table across from the crawl space, my jaw hanging open, he holds his finger to his lips, then nods hello, says he'll be back, before disappearing down the stairs to grab his morning coffee and pace up and down the street out front, smoking cigarettes and chatting people up.

This is how we become friends—or how I become Jimmy's personal ATM and chauffeur. We exchange phone numbers and make plans to listen to music at the Grand Avenue that night. He doesn't show up.

It was no great associative leap to say that Jimmy was Neal Cassady incarnate. For one thing, he never stopped talking. And it seemed like most everything he said was either pee-your-pants riotous or some deep, philosophical truth, like a soothsayer, a soothsayer with a laugh track. A shaman with a mic. When I told Jimmy that his vagabond life of riding the rails, eating in missions, and sleeping on the streets should be made into a sitcom, he immediately said, "Yeah, a sitcom called 'Honey, I'm Homeless!'"

My money and resources seemed to swiftly disappear around Jimmy. But I continued to hang around him for the hilarious things he would say. Once, when he stood me up for about the hundredth time, his excuse was that some old railroad car buddies were in town and they had insisted he drink with them all night. *Railroad car buddies.* As if he had just stepped out of a page from *The Grapes of Wrath*, on his way to the land of milk and honey. He often referred to his sexual encounters as "untying the Boy Scouts," a euphemism meant to corrupt what's wholesome or innocent, as in, "I took this high school girl who works in the store to a fancy party, a fund raiser, and after we drank wine and sampled the cheese platter, we went back to my loft and untied the Boy Scouts." I think he must say these things for the sole purpose of gauging people's reactions. Or maybe he's actually serious. I asked: "Oh, did she wear a backpack? Did she color at the table?" Jimmy once said that when he visited schools to present his poetry, his wife at the time, Marilyn, insisted on accompanying him. "Like she was afraid I'd run off with a cheerleader or something." He joked about a junior squad cheerleader being too old for him.

Jimmy was decidedly feral. He was the sort of person who would phone you up at three o'clock in the morning, on what seemed to be a drug-induced manic jag, in order to read you a poem newly scrawled out in what I imagined might be a purple crayon. Or for a more serious occasion, to bail him out of jail. It also goes without saying that despite this, or in spite of it, I liked him immediately, until the day I decided I didn't like him anymore. Or couldn't afford to. Because aside from the charming aspects of his personality, his humor, his energy, Jimmy could also, and quite often, be insufferable.

The last time I saw Jimmy was sometime just before he lost his business and left town with plans to bicycle across America. He invited me to drop by his loft to say goodbye. While I sometimes thought he might have a drug habit, I never knew for certain, but the unmistakable glass pipe and butane torch sitting atop the coffee table like a gritty still life subject confirmed my suspicions. I didn't hear from him ever again, but a few years ago I found an article on the internet from some website out of Duluth that explained how Jimmy had spent the last few years of his life living there as the unofficial barstool poet laureate.

Monday, April 3, 2004, 9:00 p.m., Burbank, CA
Jimmy leaves our table to go outside for what I assume is a smoke. Instead, he recites poetry on the street to raise money to buy us drinks and appetizers. While we sit and enjoy our panhandled drinks, our begged-for appetizer, he pens "tattoos" on himself with a Sharpie. On the knuckles of one hand he writes, "LOVE," and on the knuckles of his other hand, "HATE." On his left arm he writes, "MAMA TRIED."

My Name Is Moonbeam McSwine

1. *The Unseen Hand*

"You're all standing around like mannequins! IF SAM SHEP-
ARD WERE HERE RIGHT NOW, HE'D SHIT HIS FUCKING
PANTS!"

If John Waters needed to cast an understudy for Divine, he'd
choose Irina-the-Hun-Kaas, student-director of Sam Shepard's *The
Unseen Hand*, performed by the Footlights Ensemble at Bellevue
Community College.

"BANG!" Irina simulated the shooting of a pistol. "You're mad,
see. Really, *really* mad, okay?! Here, give me your gun." Irina took
up Trevor's pistol, while the rest of us tried to keep from laughing.
"Now, it's like this: BANG BANG BANG!" Irina strutted across
the stage in her rhinestone-studded heels and leopard-print see-
through blouse. "Okay, watch me, shoot him like *this*, BANG ..."
Gordon murmured, "Chitty, Chitty," under his breath, and right
on cue Irina finished: "Bang, Bang!" It was hilarious. "Oh shit!"
Irina set the pistol down in a panic. "Is this thing loaded?"

Irina drove a baby-blue Firebird convertible, and when she
waved goodbye in the parking lot, she looked like she was cruis-
ing down Hollywood Boulevard in a parade, a movie starlet, her
blonde ringlets stock-still from hairspray abuse.

She started a fling with Marco, the theater's distinguished
alcoholic windbag in residence. Their affair had been unofficially
announced during a cast party, when the two of them—clearly not
sticklers for discretion or ones to put on airs—niched themselves

away in a bedroom, where their exertions were well heard by all. And if anyone had any doubts that the two were an item, those were swiftly put to rest when Marco sauntered out to the party sans shirt, unbuckled pants, lit up a cigarette, and proceeded to show off the long, bloody scratches running down his back.

Two weeks later, Irina flew into a panic and dragged everyone into her drama: Marco got her pregnant. Her plight was broadcast like an Orange Alert. We all pooled our money so she could get an abortion, but she miscarried and spent all our money on drugs. Eventually, Irina and Marco were banished from the theater department after getting caught shooting up in the greenroom.

2. Li'l Abner

I pined for the role of Moonbeam McSwine. I wanted *sleeping out with hogs* to be MY line. I wanted the *fellers to squire me* only in *fine weather*. I wanted to be Moonbeam almost as much as I wanted to play the crazy cat girl Janice Vickery, from *The Effect of Gamma Rays on Man-in-the-Moon Marigolds*. Janice Vickery, who boiled the skin off a cat she supposedly got from the animal shelter and had to scrape the gristle off the joints with a knife. Janice Vickery, who wryly said, "You have no idea how difficult it is to get right down to the bones." I liked to imagine Janice Vickery not as the sociopath everyone made her out to be but as a misunderstood genius! A scientist! I wanted to play Janice Vickery as much as I wanted to play Petra from *A Little Night Music*. Petra, portrayed as the housemaid who liked to have a good time, in that good way, that fun way, her song about marrying the miller's son or maybe the businessman or maybe not anyone; maybe Petra would rather have "a wink and a wiggle and a giggle in the grass, a girl has to celebrate what passes by, there are mouths to be kissed," you know. But there was no Moonbeam for me because at fifteen, with a father who was playing the role of Earthquake McGoon, the village lech, who chased after Daisy Mae, pawed at her like a cat toy and literally *licked* her, the director wasn't willing to let me slop the hogs. I was much too innocent. So I became instead just another Dogpatcher. Certainly not Stupefying Jones! But the Dogpatcher who gets fat-shamed by Mamie: "We wants to broaden our horizons!" I squawked with my Indian corn hillbilly grin. And Mamie replied, "Yer horizons are broad enough already!"

3. *Brigadoon*

Our regular Towne Theater crowd was instructed to dress up as pagans and peasants for the Saturday night May Day Celebration. I wore my old Natalia costume from one of my Chekhov one-acts and a pink pair of ballet slippers. My father dressed as a farmer, wearing his red satin Earthquake McGoon pants with the big orange patches on the butt, and somehow he managed to herd his ornery old ram into the back of his Volvo hatchback.

"Somebody get that ram a drink!"

I never fully appreciated the kind of social cachet that livestock can bring to a hosted affair until that night, and I was reminded of it when years later my best friend, Evie, brought a Bay City Roller lookalike and his eighteen-pound boa constrictor to my house party, a literary soiree, held in honor of the first real poet I ever kissed. Really, a good hostess will never underestimate the festive potential of live reptiles—or farm animals, as my father had proved. What wine pairs with reptiles? you might ask. I found box wine to be the perfect complement.

4. *Bye Bye Birdie*

Conrad Birdie was going into the army, and I was part of a raucous chorus of idol-worshipping teenagers replete with poodle skirts and saddle shoes. I screamed so loudly and so often during the three-month run that I developed a permanent voice scorch.

During the run I acquired a boyfriend, a troubled but sweet seventeen-year-old whose Christian-conservative parents had exiled him to a halfway house with other wayward boys who also had behavioral and drug and alcohol problems. The lost boys, I call them. Boys who break into houses. Boys who rob gas stations and sell drugs. Boys who became mythic in my recollection because only in literature and films can lost boys ever hope for redemption. But I never stopped trying. I ended up losing this lost boy to a drowning accident. The last time I saw him alive, he gave me a gift—an hourglass.

5. *One Flew Over the Cuckoo's Nest*

My father co-opted one of my mother's old wigs to play Chief Bromden, the mute Indian, in *One Flew Over the Cuckoo's Nest*, for a local theater production. Although he had plenty of cultural insider awareness, he played mostly to stereotype, and his Bromden was stiff as a cigar-store Indian. I like to think he tried to bring some relevancy to the role, having been married to a Native woman, my mother, for all those years, but he was by no means a Will Sampson or Jason Momoa.

His look had the kind of blue-eyed and bronzed skin intensity often displayed by other white men playing Indians. Henry Brandon in *The Searchers* (1953). Burt Lancaster in *Apache* (1954). Iron Eyes Cody in those crying Indian commercials (1970–71). Johnny Depp in *The Lone Ranger* (2013). The list, sadly, goes on and on.

Years later my father was arrested and sent to prison, where he started up an institutional theater group. I imagine it to be called "Bards behind Bars." His letters to me mentioned his fellow inmates, his recruits—some Native, some black—and how they were studying different plays and scenes from Shakespeare and performing them to receptive audiences of their peers. *Othello, Hamlet,* and *Macbeth*. I want to know if there was a figurative

Chief Bromden or an R. P. McMurphy in residence. Maybe my father was the figurative R. P. McMurphy, sent to the Forks Correctional Facility to rouse his incarcerated colleagues from their dormancy, the catalyst who stirred things up, a trickster who changed everything.

It sounds like the makings for the perfect Hollywood movie in the vein of the white savior narrative, the all-too-familiar trope in which a heroic white character rescues folks of color from their plight. (The best exception that I can think of is Edward James Olmos in *Stand and Deliver* and maybe Morgan Freeman in *Lean on Me*.)

Movie pitch: a white savior, convicted felon, and drama teacher directs and stages Shakespearean productions with his fellow inmates. *Oz* meets *Stand and Deliver*, crossed with Kevin Costner, crossed with *The Shawshank Redemption*. Call it *Stand and Deliver a Soliloquy*. Call it *The Shakespeare Redemption*. Call it *Dances with Inmates*. Call it *Taming of the Screws*. Call it *All's Well That Ends Well in the Clink*. Call it *The Thespian of Oz*.

The Siam Sequences

The King and I

My role as Wife No. 6 means my sash is pink, I wear no crown, my feet are bare. This is all my father's idea. It started with his being cast in the Village Theater's production of *The Music Man*, followed by *Brigadoon*, and then it all flowered from there. Every three months we are in rehearsals for a new play: *The Unsinkable Molly Brown, Bye-Bye Birdie, Li'l Abner, Camelot*. One year my father borrowed one of my mother's old wigs to play Chief Bromden, the mute Indian in *One Flew Over the Cuckoo's Nest*.

My costume is a poly-cotton blend stitched together from bargain fabric, while Anna's dresses are pure flounce and flourish, epically and historically accurate: steel wire hoops, rib-crunching corsets, antique cameos and earrings, silk skirts and satin petticoats. She is the leading lady after all; she has her own dressing room, her own hair stylist, and a private voice coach. The other wives and I are relegated to dress shoulder to shoulder in a basement dungeon beneath the orchestra pit. We have to navigate a hazard of stairs shallow-stepped as a ladder. Onstage we're mere backdrops; our job is to exude quaintness, provide color, tiptoe across the stage, and endlessly smile, bow, and *wai* in supplicant fashion. "Imagine you're a lotus blossom," the choreographer directed in rehearsals. "Become the arms of a night-blooming orchid." I lose myself in this image: I am the Siam flower; the Siam flower is me. "Praise to Buddha," I sing during the *Uncle Tom's Cabin* sequence. I fly a blue river of transparent fabric over my head and pin it down with my thumbs as Simon Legree crosses its intrepid currents in pursuit of Eliza.

I have no official children, none written into the script, so I adopt Rosaria, a beautiful twelve-year-old Filipino girl who attached herself to me like a starfish the first night of rehearsals. She wears a crown; she is the King's favorite; her sash is gold lamé. Every wife covets three-year-old Amelia for their own; her father is a wealthy dentist in Mercer Island. She is blonde as Shirley Temple and never fusses or cries, even when the hair dye stings her scalp. I imagine her parents must drug her before performances or bribe her with treats because she poses on the First Wife's knee, immobile as a doll. Out of twelve children only three are Asian. Among the children are four unruly brothers, all redheaded and freckled—some nights they go onstage with their hair a patchwork of black and red like striped caterpillars. By the performance's end their eyeliner is smeared like eye black on football quarterbacks down their faces.

I am an undeterminable ethnicity, tending to blend in, more or less, in any particular group. As a child, I was assumed to belong to a family of Japanese tourists while waiting for a raft to cross over at Disneyland's Tom Sawyer's Island. At different times I wasn't allowed to play with the children of bigots. I am repeatedly asked my cultural origins as if I'm an oddity or unfathomable puzzle.

I harbor a crush on Guardsman No. 2. He works days at Champions, a costume supply store in Seattle, where I imagine he can steal all the black hair spray he needs from the store's inventory. I also have a crush on the King, the only Asian male in the entire production. The King tosses pizza dough at Pagliachi's on Broadway; I hear he did *Flower Drum Song* for the Seattle Rep, and though he isn't quite Yul Brynner or Chow Yun-fat, he's appealing to the directors for his exotic authenticity. He is topless throughout most of the performance and paints muscle definition across his breastbone with dark makeup to fill in for his modest physique. I think the director should have insisted he shave his head.

"Wah-stun peeple fuh-ni." I perform with the other wives, while Anna introduces us to alien hoopskirts and camisoles. "Too fuh-ni toobee twoo." Anna is teaching us to speak English, fold napkins, serve English tea, and slowly, through her example, challenge the King's authority, our womanly place in society; eventually, mayhem will break out through the walls of the peaceful palace, and the King will storm and sulk like a petulant child commanding beheadings and banishments.

In the real Thailand, several thousand miles away from our amateur community theater, *The King and I* is outlawed, declared illegal due to a 1930s ordinance that prohibits any portrayal of the Thai monarchy. People are routinely flogged not by police but by their fellow citizens if caught not standing during Nationalist anthems. Unlike Great Britain's routine media lampooning of their monarchy, caricature sketches of the Thai monarchy in the local papers is nonexistent. A citizen cracking jokes about the King at the local watering hole is unheard of, unless it's an expatriate like my father.

In the Village Theater's production of the *King and I*, most everyone is Caucasian. They cover their heads with black hair spray, paint elongated and exaggerated lines across their eyelids, and lavish their skin with ethnic-colored stage makeup. The wives are properties of royalty but conversely are costumed in the tackiest and cheapest of fabric. I carpool with a Japanese woman whose husband is a Chinese jeweler and owns a reputable shop in an upscale shopping mall in Bellevue. Her little daughter's favorite food is escargot—not McDonald's, certainly not dim sum, but *snails*.

All of this is years before Jody Foster and Chow Yun-fat were banned from filming in Thailand—years before I imagined my father would live twenty-two air hours away in Southeast Asia and years before I even knew where and what Siam was.

Soi Buakhao

My first morning in Pattaya, I was lifted from sleep by an argument in halted, rudimentary English between a Thai prostitute, her pimp, and a john. It was five in the morning, the light just beginning to rise, a pale wash of pinks and oyster-grays in the sky outside my window. Initially, I thought the disturbance was a fatigued dream aroused from my twenty-two hours of travel, but as the argument in the hallway grew louder and the drunken john more unruly and insistent, I tumbled out of my lucid dream into the shock of the new day. They were arguing about money, or rather, the drunk man was trying to worm his way out of paying. The pimp sounded like an oriental wise man dispelling ancient Chinese secrets or fortune cookie proverbs; he was so reasonable and calm, almost smug. "You pay girl one thousand baht—this is what you agree to."

The john continued to protest in a garbled English I could barely make out; when he spoke, he sounded like he was swallowing his tongue. Intermittently, the Thai girl would pipe in with her protests, a mix of Thai and English. It was easy enough to make out her argument—she just wanted her damn money. The wise man pimp intoned in his caramel-calm voice, "You fuck her; you pay." It was comforting to know the word *fuck* crossed all barriers of country and culture; it was a universal and all-purpose word, like McDonald's golden arches, instantly recognized throughout the world.

I was staying in a very nice hotel, very clean, in fact just newly built and conveniently located across the courtyard from my father's apartment. My room had auspicious amenities: leather couch, gleaming tiles, lovely draperies, full-sized fridge, thirty-inch television, *blessed* air conditioner. It was more expensive than the original hotel my father led me to the night before, but I refused that arrangement for its shabbiness, its unclean look, its lack of an elevator. The newer, twelve-dollar-a-night hotel with its bright, shiny interiors wasn't the sort of place one would immediately associate with prostitution, yet most of the tenants were prostitutes or foreign johns on holiday. The rooms didn't have that seedy underworld panache because in places like Pattaya, a city that was originally founded to entertain World War II servicemen on leave, there is no underworld, nothing to hide. What you see is what you get. I've never had very strong convictions against prostitution, yet I'm not ignorant to its perils either, especially in the third world countries, where the reality is more along the lines of white slavery and not the almost noble-sounding "world's oldest profession." Of course, my father's take on prostitution, being the misogynist and unabashed bigot that he is, borders on the profane and absurd. He once married his long-term Thai "girlfriend" for permanent citizenship. She was totally deaf and moonlighted in professional female wrestling. Most of my father's peers have also married Thai prostitutes. They don't view themselves as imperialists and corruptors; they view themselves as furthering a depressed economy, helping the peasants, delivering the hill tribe girls from lives of hauling water and harvesting rice.

The hallway voices seemed to have reached some agreeable arrangement because I heard doors slam and footprints clip down the hallway. I showered in the tiled room, amazed at its abundant ergonomics and practicality. I dressed and spent the early morning hours touring the city streets near my hotel. It was still morning-dark; people were moving about at neither a brisk pace nor at a languishing pace but somewhere in between, like sea anemones or ribbons of seaweed waving in shallow pools of water. Bar girls fled home on motorbikes, throngs of them dotted the pavement, appearing as wilted prom flowers in a dilapidated parade. I captured a photograph of barefoot monks in flowing orange robes selecting their breakfast fruits from the open markets. They made polite attempts to barter for star fruits and mangoes, but I noticed the vendors smiled at them and refused their money. It is strictly prohibited for women to touch them, and it is customary for all young men to practice a monastic life as a rite of passage in much the same way that young men in post-midcentury America were expected to serve time in the military.

I walked. I passed bookstores for *farangs*, the Thai word for "foreigners," which reminds me of the name for the horrible-looking creatures with the overly large ears in *Star Trek's Next Generation*—Ferengis. My father expressed astonishment when I purchased new paperbacks. They are the only commodity that is not priced obscenely low; they cost nearly the same as books in America. I bought weathered copies of *Angela's Ashes* and *House of Sand and Fog* for my father from an outdoor vendor. I had to unearth the copies from beneath a pile of comic book digests, the main literary diet among the locals. I passed open stalls and small air-conditioned grocery and sundry stores. Cyber cafés are all the rage, and they're on every corner, along with 7-11s. Stray dogs dominated the streets, especially at the early hour, mating and scavenging. There were massive piles of coconut husks; it was someone's job to spend twelve hours a day, six to seven days a week, cracking them open, extracting the firm white meat, and discarding the unwanted husks. Someone's failed business was literally going up in flames; they did not waste time demolishing the stick, rubber, and tin constructions but just set them on fire to make room for something else. I watched them burn, smoke stretching its arms into the hazy sky. I crossed the streets, a tricky negotiation against a delta of small diesel engines, a wager in blue smoke and peril. In Arab Town an albino child played tag while nearby a black crow of a woman in full burka demanded my attention. I walked for nearly two hours up Soi Buakhao, my clothes stuck to me, the morning lush as rising cream.

Vowel Movements

I soon discover that my dark hair offers me passport among the locals. There are two prices, a sliding scale, one for natives and one for *farangs*. I can ride the blue pickup taxies for five baht, the bus routes for fifty, depending on how far I'm going. One late evening at my hotel, a drunken Brit surprised me from behind, grasping me around the waist, confusing me for his rented companion. At the time I was trying to secure a plunger from the night desk clerk. It was 2:00 a.m., and I was gesturing wildly, scribbling cartoon commodes on tourist brochures, playing a late-night game of charades. I hadn't bothered with buying a translation book. I didn't have the foggiest notion what the Thai word for *plunger* is, and from the desk clerk's puzzled expression it seemed such things did not exist. It was crucial I get one. My toilet was backed up, an embarrassment, to say the least, because at 2:00 a.m., with no simple word for *plunger*, the courtyard populated with motor scooter cabbies, a night watchman I nicknamed Cockeye for his lazy eye, and a drunken Brit who thought I was his girlfriend, the *big one* caught in the plumbing like a walleyed pike wasn't exactly my crowning glory in that moment.

I am an American. Everything I know is mega-large, super-sized: big trucks, big talk, big bombs, big money, and in that moment, as everyone in the courtyard and in the two neighboring hotels that faced each other knew, big stools. The desk clerk shouted across the courtyard to the Lake Apartments' clerk; the Lake Apartments' clerk shouted back. They called back and forth across the courtyard, the Asian piazza, for what seemed an eternity until someone was presumably woken up to unlock the custodian's closet. The desk clerk assured me, "Five minutes, five minutes," and I returned to my room, where just moments later Cockeye was standing in my doorway, smiling and prepared to pull double duty. I *waied* and brushed him away, my face heated, mouth pursed.

There were nice times to blend in, like when I was riding the taxi or trying to remain unnoticed by the bogus jewelry salesmen on the lookout for easy marks, but this was not one of those times. I overtipped the night watchman. My big fat American dollars went far.

Lessons in Thai

How much? *Tow rye (ka)?*

In the market tent she holds out her calculator, exacts your baht to the shilling. Her wares include a basket of yellow kittens.

Smile? *Yim my (ka)?*

Too often they scowl at you, contrary to the guidebook's assertions that you are in the land of a quaint people, the land of smiles and goodwill. The guidebook was undoubtedly written pre-9/11.

Thank you. *Khorp khoon mak na (ka).*

To the pannier cook, the peasant shack lady, the bar girls who shared their fermented baby crabs, the housekeeper, the laundry girls, the coconut ice cream vendor, and the waitress at the Cheers bar.

Along the Waterfront Promenade

I am convinced anything's for sale. I eye the Nazi helmets, assorted skinhead paraphernalia, brass knuckles and steel knives. There are Bin Laden T-shirts emblazoned with his image as if he's a hero or god.

"I dare you to wear that through the airport," my father says.

Hidden in the back of the reproduction painting salon is a poster-sized canvas of Hitler framed in walnut-stained wood.

My father waxes nostalgic for the good ol' days, fifteen years earlier, when the beachfront boardwalks and promenades and the famous Marine Bar hosted snake charmers and fire breathers, circus dancers and nude contortionists. A time when certain clubs served the most heinous of appetites: public defecation served on platters, a fetish smorgasbord, a regular isle of Hades before the morality police ruined everyone's good and perverse fun.

"Now it's all baby strollers and Walt Disney. Family values. They've cleaned up the streets to be palatable to dimple-bottomed Norwegian ladies on holiday."

There was a time I argued with my father over this kind of thing. My sympathies used to cry out for the poor girls forced into prostitution, mere children, fleeing from the hill country to earn money for their families. He denied all reports; the British documentaries I'd viewed in cinema houses in the University District were always slanted and exaggerated in his estimation.

"They *enjoy* the lifestyle. They're hustlers and thieves. They get off on it. They know how to take advantage of a lonely *farang*. They can get him to go through his travel funds and then disappear before the poor slob figures out what hit him."

I see the girls everywhere. So often they are paired with the homeliest of men. Men without teeth, brash-voiced Aussies, the over-loud Germans; the jaundiced and decrepit, men with copper hooks for hands, men with spinal injuries. And half of the prostitutes aren't even girls but beautifully made-up trans performers—a very lucrative industry of the area but one that makes my father livid.

In the tourist district the shop girls crowd the customers. They disrupt my shopping haze with concerned and overly helpful expressions. They hold out assorted oddities: ashtrays shaped like penises, framed monarch butterflies, cheap satin robes touted as silk, live hamsters, and the occasional offers of gold.

One day I disappear to Arab Town. I meet the limbless woman who sits all day at the gates of the shopping mall. A faux airplane is staged as a crash into the neck of the building, a marquee for Ripley's Believe It or Not Museum. I buy a Coke and rest from the heat, sitting on a bench along a stretch of Saudi restaurants. An Arab man joins me, even though there are other benches available. His body is uncomfortably close, too close. His voice calls to a colleague across the sidewalk court; his butt maneuvers for more of my bench. He is touching me now, bullying me from the bench. I ignore him and leave. I stroll up the street.

My father, who does not discriminate in his racial bigotry but who pretty much thinks everyone deserves his contempt, had warned me about Arabs. He tried to convince me that only a few years ago, Thais posted NO ARABS ALLOWED signs like a Jim Crow law, prohibiting them from select restaurants and clubs. I don't believe it.

This is all much too strange for me.

The man who took over my bench. The limbless woman begging for rice. The hamsters that appear otherworldly. The colliding heat, exhaust, and disco music spilling out from the quarters of Boys' Town. The casual regard for prostitution. The Ripley's Believe It or Not Museum's marquee.

At Nong Nooch Tropical Gardens
The Ukrainians climb the tigers like playground seesaws. The big cats are too fat to care—what's a spike heel pressed to its rib? Just another day in the mines. What bother can an infant's head be offered at the jaws of a lion; it's all the same to her—meat on a stick or something to paw; a round, blonde toy that drools and coughs. Here the elephants must earn their keep painting pre-

school art for the tourists. I suppose the chimps must get jealous; they're the ones with the opposable thumbs after all. What good is a sloppy trunk when they can play Tchaikovsky with their feet? Hammer away like a nickelodeon for one thin ticket or a cluster of ripe bananas.

There are places on this Earth so magical that they have the power to irrevocably alter your DNA—re-sequence your helix coils until you resemble a large egg or the fine, soft down slick on the face of an orchid. Some people think Disneyland holds the key; others think a condo in Maui does or the Sistine Chapel. But on this day I fell madly in love with an orangutan. He *listens* like no one else ever did; he makes me laugh! I want to bear his little orange children, eat tamarinds and butternuts, swing like a lemur from gum trees forever.

My father chain-smokes Chinese tobacco beneath an umbrella of palms. He says the difference between Thailand and yogurt is that yogurt has culture. He enjoys being provocative. It used to rile me up but not any longer. I just pretend that I'm vacationing with Hunter S. Thompson and it all works out in the end. What he means by culture is high art, a Western aesthetic, not comic books and lounging Buddha's drenched in acres of gold but relics from the Age of Enlightenment, baroque artifacts, Grecian texts, the Renaissance.

He is my learned father, my genetic sire, fingerprint of all my thoughts, every breath's spectacle. He is an unabashed imperialist, Caliban's keeper and Friday's Crusoe. He is a firm believer in a superior race, and nothing I can ever say or do will save him.

Houndstooth Jacket

Ever since I received the email that my father had died, I have been carrying around his high school graduation photo. In it he is wearing a wool houndstooth jacket—a jacket that holds some sort of spell over him. Perhaps it represented finer times, those moments before disappointment overtook his worldview. I find myself showing the photo to strangers. "Look, this is my father," I'll say, as if I'm awaiting absolution for loving him. "I used to wear that suit coat in my teens." And I'll add, "With legwarmers and a sequined headband." As if that makes it more significant.

The last time I visited him in Thailand, he asked me to take the jacket. I knew why he wanted me to take it. I knew he didn't have plans to stick around much longer. I didn't want to acknowledge that sobering possibility—the idea that he knew something I didn't. My mother had just died, and my grandmother only three months later, and I was much too wrung out to be burdened with anticipating another's death. He knew that. And sought to protect me.

The last time I saw him we were saying goodbye in an airline taxi at dawn after we'd stayed up all night watching American late-night talk shows and waiting for a pizza that was never delivered. I sat weeping in the plane, waiting nearly two hours for takeoff until our delay was finally announced—the baggage handlers had earlier collided into the loading door. We spent the rest of the afternoon wading through customs, relinquishing our passports to authorities, forgoing our luggage, being dosed with restaurant tokens and herded into a five-star airport hotel for an overnight stay. I tried phoning my father several times but couldn't get ahold of him. I wanted so much to spend more time with him.

One more night. I wanted one more night.

All of his burdens and life disappointments I corralled onto my own shoulders during my three-week visit. Pity is not an emotion that is easily relinquished. I told myself that he made his choices, that I couldn't impose my own values upon him, that he had lived life according to his own conditions, made no compromises; that he had swung from chandeliers, lived like a king and a hedonist, and examined more of life's intricacies and fallacies than most people ever have the fortitude or curiosity for. But I still felt pity.

Even now, when I've removed myself from the minutiae of his passing, when the hospital will inevitably follow some protocol for itinerant expats and unceremoniously incinerate the remains, I am removed from all that. I am removed from any decorum or ritual.

Just three months prior to receiving the overseas email, I had a dream: I arrived to my home, and my father has packed up all my belongings for a move I desperately did not want.

"But I'm *happy*. Don't make me leave!" My dream self protested.

I finally put my father's ashes into my storage locker after almost two weeks of entombing him in the trunk of my car. I don't like picking up the box . . . an odd mix of revulsion and sorrow. I have been having a delayed reaction regarding his passing. Initially, in April, I was so wound up emotionally in other things that it didn't faze me. Now I have time for it to faze me. And though I'm not overwhelmed particularly, I am feeling stabs of regret that are best described as FUCKFUCKFUCK.

A month from this day a coconut ice cream vendor will be wearing Dad's houndstooth jacket during the flash of a rainstorm. He will pull the collar up against his neck, ride his operation beneath an awning, and reach in the front pocket for a package of cigarettes. He will light up and inhale the smooth smoke into his lungs. He will look for the portentous shapes in the cloudburst. He will imagine the dark loaves of his wife's thighs. He will examine his life, give praise to Buddha, and he will be content even without reminding himself to be content. A quick smile will play across his mouth, as the unbidden image of an elephant in a rain slicker crosses his mind. When the rain lets up, he will visit the waterfront promenade. He will buy a red rose for his daughter. And tomorrow he will teach her to pray.

III

Micro
(Aggression)
Memoirs

First World (Story) Problems
Brown Girl Multiple Choice Edition

1. If a person on Facebook posts an illustration of a slave ship's cargo hold filled with hundreds of African people in an attempt to convey how horrifying modern day airline travel has become—especially transatlantic flights to Paris!—how many minutes should you wait, letting that sink in, before you call bullshit?

    a. No minutes. You should respond immediately! It's your duty to educate white folks everywhere. How else will they ever learn to be culturally sensitive allies?

    b. No minutes. Just shake it off and keep scrolling.

    c. Eat a cupcake; you'll feel better.

2. "Sally" works as a cashier at a drugstore. One day her supervisor "Barb" gestures toward a Native woman who is browsing ten feet away. When Sally's supervisor mutters, "Gotta watch those people like a hawk," should Sally:

    a. Ignore her supervisor—it must just be a misunderstanding.

    b. Inform her supervisor that the Native woman she's referring to just so happens to be Sally's mother, who is visiting her at work and waiting for her to go on break.

    c. Internalize the interaction, add it to a hundred and a thousand other similar incidents since childhood, and slowly, accreted over time, suspend Sally's faith and trust in her fellow humans while increasing her sense of self-condemnation.

Is it reasonable for Sally to hold endless arguments with herself about how she's overreacting, being overly sensitive, "playing the race card"; how no one actually means her any harm, not really, and how she should feel grateful, making mental note after mental note that no one likes a complainer, that no one will like her if she complains about situations and incidents that condemn others and might paint them in unflattering ways and/or, worst, as bigots or racists? Is she a professional victim? Who does she think she is, anyway? Rosa Parks?

  d. Calm down.

3. At another chain store Sally once worked for, the manager called her into the front office "for a little powwow," where she proceeded to:

  a. Congratulate her!
  b. Offer her a raise!
  c. Fire her.

If you answered c, could this be considered a microaggression if the manager wasn't aware that Sally was Native? Because Sally didn't wear braids or wear a headdress or other feather-fringe accessories? Because Sally" didn't have a medicine bag or carry a bow and arrow, and she didn't paddle a birchbark canoe to work or ride in on a spotted pony but mostly just kind of blended in with regular society, so how would the manager know? She didn't.

4. A Pulitzer Prize–winning poet who wrote books about slavery, the antebellum era, and civil rights visited the very homogeneous graduate writing program. One evening after a reading, the graduate students took the poet to a bar outside of town for karaoke. Was the bar called:

a. Rudy's.

b. The Slurp 'n' Burp.

c. The Plantation.

5. The preeminent writers' conference accepts a panel that seems to be based upon a kind of fatally false but persistently constructed, fabricated, colonialist, shrink-wrapped New Agey Leanin' Tree fantasy Indian paint-by-number chicanery set, which the white supremacist narrative insists on doling out and swilling down ad nauseam. Did the panel description include:

a. Fairies.

b. Pirates.

c. Rainbows.

d. Unicorns.

e. Keebler Elves.

f. Four Eastern Woodlands Indigenous writers reading poetry and prose anthologies, evoking the nineteenth-century ghost dance that Native people once did to take a stand for their lives and defy vanishing forever. These twenty-first-century word warriors read work that embodies how the ghost dance prevails in their poems and stories that shine on in affirmation of Mother Earth, the spirits, and the ancient beauty ways.

6. The Academy Awards have earned a faithful hashtag following, #OscarsSoWhite. So, when in 2017 the wrong film was presented for the Oscar for Best Picture, incorrectly presented to *La La Land* instead of *Moonlight*, in my own mind it was not unprecedented and seemed to represent something sinister. Why would I have any reason to be mistrustful of an error?

a. Because when author Daniel Handler presented African American author Jacqueline Woodson a National Book

Award for her poetic memoir *Brown Girl Dreaming*, he "joked" about her being allergic to watermelon.

b. Because when Sean Penn presented Alejandro González Iñárritu's Oscar for *Birdman*, he said, "Who gave this son of a bitch his green card?"

c. Because when Supreme Court justice John Roberts reworded the oath swearing in President Obama so it was necessary to swear him in again later, all the news headlines stated that Obama had flubbed up his lines, when it was Justice Roberts who was in error.

d. Because the award went to *La La Land*'s producer for being "so gracious," and *Moonlight* was robbed of its moment.

7. For many Indigenous people the holidays and observance days are psychic landmines and a constant reminder that Native people are a colonized people whose own rich and complex history and culture mean very little, if anything, within the broader society. Which holidays are potentially offensive to Indigenous people?

a. Halloween.
b. Thanksgiving.
c. Columbus Day.
d. Independence Day.
e. All of the above.
f. All 365 days of the year.

8. How many white supremacists does it take to change a light bulb?

a. The white supremacist has to want to change.
b. Society has to change.
c. First, you need a ladder.

Tweets as Assigned Texts for a Native American Studies Course

On Sovereignty

- T-shirt slogan: SOVEREIGNTY RULES!

On Environment and Land

- White people. The original manspreaders. Manspreading the North American continent since 1492.
- "I grew up in a region of diverse geographic splendor called Snoqualmie, which is the Indian word for 'beautiful mountain colonized by assholes.'"

On History

- "Let them eat fry bread." — Colonialism
- Film pitch: Native woman gets up off couch, drives to mall to buy light bulbs and rotisserie chicken. Journey of intrigue and discovery.
- Settlers put the *colon* in *colonialism.*

On Political Activism

- Bitch, please, Iktome is way more kickass than your fucking Spider-Man.
- Last night I attended my anger management support group: Idle No More.
- It seems that a hallmark of "Native humor" is the posting of funny memes on social media that respond to water

protectors being attacked by dogs less than twenty-four hours after actually having been attacked by dogs.

- This afternoon I visited local cafés and demanded that everyone speak Nimipuutimt or else I'd call ICE on their immigrant-colonialist-settler asses.

On Racism and Social Justice

- Bank teller at Wells Fargo was wearing a Cleveland Indians Chief Wahoo ball cap. Casual Friday or racist Friday?
- Resolve to say, "You know nothing, Jon Snow," whenever someone with white privilege condescends to me.
- A woman I've never met asked me if I was Native American, so I told her yes and asked her age and weight.

On Feminism

- The term *Indigenous feminist* is redundant.
- There are many books centered on Indigenous feminine empowerment. I'm waiting for one titled TRILL. Indigenous women invented feminism; we have been "li-li-li-li-li-li-li-li-ing" from time immemorial.
- Does this ribbon skirt make me look like a nonstandard beauty archetype steeped in gender-biased ideologies propagated by antiquated and oppressive systems of patriarchy?
- What's the Lakota word for *intersectional feminism*? Is it just an emoji of a knife?

On Identity Politics

- I will fight no more about blood quantum forever. —Chief Joseph reboot
- What's your rez cred score?

- Thinking about enrolling in the Ginger Tribe for the government-subsidized sunscreen.
- When people say they identify as a "white-passing person of color," it makes me think of intestinal gas.

On Spirituality
- Just for fun I like to put travel-size lotions in donation baskets at church.
- As a Native American wordsmith, I use *every* part of the sacred sentence.
- For a thousand dollars I'll teach you sacred Native American rituals. The first cleansing rite involves you, a brush, ammonia, and my kitchen floor.

On Food
- The Native Americans ate the *hole* part of the buffalo.
- It's a rez-dog eat rez-dog world.
- Saw a bumper sticker that said: "BEEF: Because the West wasn't won on salad." For an indigenous person it might as well have said, "I support genocide."
- Whenever someone uses the term *manspreader*, I think about soft cheeses.

On Media and Technology
- Tele–Vision Quest now in HD.
- TV show pitch: sitcom about a tribal court judge named Ruth, called "The Whole Ruth & Nothing but the Ruth."
- A friend said *The Revenant* was a journey into the heart-of-darkness war movie. I agree: Apocalypse Powwow.
- The ancestors have very straightforward and sensible protocols about texting, sexting, and social media status updating. It's in the handbook.

On Relationships
- Finally got my official home-wrecker merit badge from the Skank Scouts.
- When another Native person unfriends you on Facebook, you're like 7-Up—the un-*kola*.
- Stands with a Stiffy is a good name for a Comanche warrior protagonist who is torn between his people and his desire for the fiery damsel Petunia.
- "Indigeneity" always makes me think "giggity giggity."

On Art and Literature
- Literary journal I'd like to see: *Crabs in a Bucket Review*.
- Two things always present in classic western literature: death and tragedy. By that logic there should be hundreds of Great Native American Novels.
- I'm the Ron Jeremy of Native American literature—I'm that good. Fight me.
- Sadly, I feel that until I can play "Folsom Prison Blues" on the ukulele in front of Panda Express wearing a bustier and a pink tutu, my identity as a poet is trash.

On Representation in Popular Culture
- "You're not the Indian Lady Gaga, you know." "Yes I *am*!" Runs crying hysterically from room.
- For Halloween I wore a Disney's Pocahontas outfit and went as a racist.
- *The Real Rez Wives of Nez Perce County*.

On Indigenous Lifeways
- How do you say *velociraptor* in Lakota?

- The annual Inter-Tribal Alliteration Powwow was spectac-ularly replete with buckskins, braids, beads, and bustles, no booze and no beer.
- Luke Warmwater is in my shower, and I'm waiting for a plumber to come over. Today my life is a risqué powwow MC over a loudspeaker.

On Fashion

- "All this talk about the depth and richness of his skin made me think she wanted to make a skin suit from his hide." "Yeah. Buffalo Jill."
- How do you say *ugly Christmas sweater* in Lakota?

On Pretendians

- In a future version of *The Hunger Games*, if Natives are all rounded up, will Andrea Smith volunteer like Katniss, as tribute, to save my life?
- "Pretendians give off mixed smoke signals."

Ghoul, Interrupted

1.

Do we fear demons? Or do we fear possession? I remember scenes in *The Exorcist*: demon girl creeping down the staircase like a spider; demon girl's head spinning like a top; demon girl announcing death to all, then peeing on the floor. Demon girl *clearly* out of control. Demon girl is prepubescent, premenstrual, hormonal! The patriarchy is powerless and must pronounce demon girl demonically possessed. But is she? What's the cultural message? (*The patriarchy made me do it?*) The social consciousness's fear of burgeoning womanhood? Women on the verge; girls with urges, hormonal surges, and sex splurges? It is the horror of the whore, the female body in revolt, boy toy exploits? Feminine foibles.

2.

I was eight when my altruistic and supposedly socially conscious parents took in fifteen-year-old foster "child" Jerry. It was December 1973—Merry Christmas! And *The Exorcist* had just been released. Our new foster child Jerry boasted about having seen the movie, and one of his favorite ways to impress my sister and me was to detail particulars of especially gruesome scenes as if describing the aftermath of a car accident. He recounted the horrors blow by blow. Vividly. He also laid the groundwork for monumental pranks. One of them involved rigging my mother's dresser with strings and wires to slam the bedroom door shut after she entered the room. Another involved me lying in bed spitting pea soup and speaking some approximation of Latin or Tongues. The pranks never panned out, but Jerry did manage to get his shit together enough to paint *The Exorcist* in red paint across the side of the backyard playhouse.

3.

I have read feminist critiques on movies like *The Exorcist, Carrie*, and *The Exorcism of Emily Rose*, and they all seem to view the "demon" as a symbol for female sexuality—"Demons are a girl's best friend," one article surmised. The critiques point to the terror men throughout the centuries must have felt when confronted with feminine power, which explains the Salem witch trials, which explains honor killings, which explains foot binding and corsets. Not to mention infanticide, veiling, and the Dallas Cowboy Cheerleaders.

4.

My first viewing of *The Exorcist* occurred sometime in high school in the basement TV room of a friend's house, and ever since I've been haunted by unbidden images of possessed Regan MacNeil floating in her pea soup–stained nightgown while the priests shout, "The power of Christ compels you!" For years, decades! such images have come to mind when I rise from the warmth of my bed to visit the bathroom. Flick goes the light, and the threat lessens; the demon girl scrambles back into the ether. It is this monster-bogeyman that has forged itself into my neural pathways. This realization has been revelatory actually, a breakthrough.

Part of the reason for my indelible imaginings probably has something to do, if not everything to do, with our foster child's habitual haunting of my own prepubescent burgeoning. I wasn't in danger of being possessed by demons but of having my virginity possessed by the fifteen-year-old sex maniac my parents deemed appropriate to live in our house. Not a day would go by when Jerry didn't pin me down and torment me, when my developing breasts weren't the topic of discussion, when roughhousing always seemed to serve as just an excuse to feel me up. I developed early for my age, and Jerry taught me that it was not a casual event but that it should elicit special attention. A lot of special attention.

5.

It was the 1970s. Words like *rape* and *pedophilia* had not appeared in the national dialogue yet. I wasn't especially alert to the idea that what Jerry was doing to me was necessarily rapey or pervy. He was just a kid, much like me, except that he was older, a teenager. So, for these reasons I never thought to tell my parents about it. I thought it was normal. Maybe if I hadn't fought him off, put up resistance, he might have taken things further. He wasn't the first adolescent boy who put his hands on me in that way. During visits to my mom's rez, left behind at the house while the adults went off to do whatever it was adults went away at night to do, my much older cousin, like sixteen or older, on the pretense of being cold and wanting to cuddle up inside my sleeping bag with me for warmth, shoved his hand down my underwear, explored whatever it was he felt it necessary to explore. This felt unwelcome and threatening, a personal invasion, and he stopped after I pushed him away. But what if he didn't stop? Or if Jerry didn't stop?

Maybe if sexual predation was a Judy Blume book, I would have known differently, known it was wrong. Maybe if it was an *Afterschool Special* or an episode of the *Brady Bunch*, I would have responded differently—told my mother, for instance, told anyone. We were not having those kinds of conversations when I was growing up, and despite my sixth grade class introducing sex ed in the curriculum, only the basics were ever covered. I always wondered how my parents could sit in a theater for two hours viewing a film with a demon girl masturbating with a crucifix but broaching the topic of sex was off the table for family hour.

6.

Jerry continued living at our house for the remainder of the school year, occasionally disappearing for two- to three-day stretches, until my father must have realized Jerry's rehabilitation was futile, that he wasn't going to turn into an Eagle Scout overnight. So, my father returned him to whatever puppy farm he was rescued from. It was years later that I told my father about Jerry's abuse. I've come to realize that it is the image of Regan MacNeil that serves as a symbol for my lost innocence. She haunts me. But is it ever too late to have the perfect childhood?

7.

What if instead of the perfect Princesses franchise, Disney launched a campaign for the Anti-Princesses. Rather than fearing Regan MacNeil's possession and all the other possessed girls from the oeuvre of possessed prepubescent girl films, Disney capitalized on reality for a damn sec. Imagine the merchandise! The Anti-Princess Theme Park. Ugly Stepsister bedsheets. Regan lunchbox replete with demon head twist-off cap thermos. Carrie White tampons and training bras for those "dirty pillows." Nightgowns with your favorite possessed girl printed down the front. Give me the underbelly of disenchantment, the un-glittered, un-pink, un-speckled. As much as I wanted to be a Disney Princess, as much as I admired Cinderella and Snow White and Sleeping Beauty, a part of me was ruined for that. I never identified with the Princesses, preferring instead the stepsister, the wicked queens, the Ouija Board–curious girl. As repellent and frightening as they were, I must have known I wouldn't be, or couldn't be, the otherwise untouched, unspoiled, perfect tiara-wearing Princess.

IV

Garsh Durn It! You Say Patriarchy, I Say Patri-
Malarkey, Dollars to Donuts Cuckoo Banana Pants,
You Gals & Your Lady Power This 'n' That

An Open Letter to White Women Concerning *The Handmaid's Tale* and America's Historical Amnesia

Dear Barron, Dakota, Jezebel, Brontë, Caprice, Cher, et al.,

I don't mean to single anyone out here, but as an Indigenous woman, it behooves me to point out that while I perfectly understand your fondness for *The Handmaid's Tale* as a white feminist anthem, I can't help but feel all somehow about it. Each week when all of you are discussing and posting recaps of the latest episode on Facebook, etc., I'm resisting the urge to cram my face into the couch pillows to keep from screaming. I don't mean to point blame at anyone, per se, but I'm talking to you, Katniss, Guinevere, and Fig.

You see, Veronica, while *The Handmaid's Tale* presents a dystopian world ruled by a white totalitarian and fascist regime and while it appears to bear at least some similarity to our current conservative administration, Reese, and as entertaining as *The Handmaid's Tale* is for consumers of premium television and popular culture, Madison, might I offer a reminder that the Republic of Gilead is in fact fictional. And at least for the time being, Fleur, white women are not being forcibly recruited into brothels or radioactive work farms or used as baby-making vessels for the Republic.

But if I may be so bold, do you know what's actually *not* fictional, Kinsey? *The Indian Maiden's Tale.* Yes, Indigenous women are well acquainted with that American dystopian nightmare, and at the risk of sounding like old-broomstick-up-her-ass Aunt Lydia, an episode from *The Indian Maid-*

en's Tale is when Indigenous children were torn from their mothers and confined to residential boarding schools, forced to contend with all manner of horrors and abuses—a hellscape of horrors and abuses, not so very different from those portrayed in your favorite TV programming. So, I hope that the next time you tune into Hulu, Waverly, you'll pause and think about Indigenous women and children who endured unconscionable suffering.

And during commercial breaks, Fiona, may I also remind you that Indigenous women suffer violence and rape at astonishing rates: the Department of Justice in 2016 reported that 56 percent of the two thousand women surveyed had experienced sexual violence. And if that doesn't have you reaching for the smelling salts, Eloise, sterilization of Indigenous women was a rampant practice; the U.S. General Accounting Office reported that the Indian Health Service sterilized 3,406 Indigenous women between 1973 and 1976. And according to a report compiled by the Lakota People's Law Project, Lark, Indigenous women are incarcerated at six times the rate of white women. I hope you'll think of that the next time Offred debases herself by saying, "Blessed be the fruit," or Mrs. Waterford sits pensively in her blue frock in her blue room thinking about how miserable her life is and how she wants to disappear right into the fucking wallpaper forever.

As entertaining as *The Handmaid's Tale* is for fans of Orwellian, nihilistic programming, Betsy, it does not represent all of society. But it does effectively represent the cultural and historical amnesia of America, Saffron. And maybe you will switch to the History Channel and watch an episode of *The Indian Maiden's Tale* instead, Hyacinth.

Sincerely,
Tiffany Midge

Fertility Rites

At age nine I discovered a pond full of tadpoles in the woods behind the newly built Heather Glen Family Estates. No frogs to kiss and seek my fortune with, just the blind pale swimmers—all heads and tails flapping in the algae muck. I transplanted them to buckets on the back porch, careful to re-create their new home to replicate their old; hauling water from the pond, transplanting moss, grass, pus-yellow swamp rot. I marveled at their design, their spongy slickness, the way they glided and wiggled from one wall of the bucket habitat to the next, with no apparent destination, no goal but to grow into frogs. This is what I hoped for—buckets of bullfrogs and horny toads who made deep-throated calls, courting the twilight. This is what I anticipated, meaty legs to harvest and sell, to pickle in old mayonnaise jars.

But the tadpoles always died.

Even replenishing their pond water daily with fresh pond water didn't help. I brought back more tadpoles, but after a couple of days, they would die too; I had disrupted a fragile ecosystem and couldn't re-create it like the aphid experiments in Mrs. Louden's science class or the rain forest habitat at the Woodland Park Zoo. The pond was an abundant, all-giving womb, a not-to-be-messed-with mother of crawdads, beetles, and dragonflies. And I was a failed incubator, a mad scientist tempting nature and fate, in danger of throwing it all out of balance, sealing my fate with every unintended murder. Today, at this stage of life, I don't have children, nor will I ever, and I can't help wondering about karma—all those ruined tadpoles, all those poor bastard frogs.

I think of the tadpoles when I think of mushroom hunting. How last fall I met Mary, a devout amateur mycologist, just as she was mid-grope for a cluster of flabby white fruits out at the hillsides by Lake Padden. She likes to defy the guidebooks, playing Russian roulette with her liver and schools of cataloged toxins.

"The guidebooks say they are poisonous, but they haven't been for me," she says, and I hope these won't be the words etched on her tombstone.

The State of Alaska's epidemiology bulletin titled *Hazards of Stalking the Wild Mushroom* lists common myths about mushrooms. The first old wives' tale being poisonous mushrooms tarnish a silver spoon. I've been with men like that. Men who tarnished confidence, tainted weeklong intakes of breath saved just for them. Men who were listed in all the field manuals but were overlooked or purposely disregarded just like the hapless characters from a *Lifetime* movie. It should be that easy: testing your potential mates like scraping a diamond across glass or placing a canary into a mineshaft.

I disclosed my secret spot to Mary—a smorgasbord of flesh-toned corals—and she promised she wouldn't touch my pet Stropharia, coveted for its cap skirted with lace tatting like a canopy bed. She scrambled down an embankment, thinking she'd spied a mass of chicken fried mushrooms; she was so cavalier uprooting a specimen, a Jonquil Amanita, just to show me where its cap once met its stem, where the wings now flapped uselessly as skin tags. She stroked the shaft teasingly, then tossed it aside, declaring it "no good—it's poisonous," as if she were pronouncing the fate of a eunuch. Her disregard bothered me, this casual evacuation of a mushroom that had grown as large as my hand, through five nights of rain, its genesis a sprite-like exchange of spores and rot,

chancing the elements, the hazards of mollusks, to break open
through the soil like the fist of a prizefighter—like the gold-painted
Leggs pantyhose egg
hidden from view in the spring grass in the field behind the library,
one of five prize eggs that the teachers had secreted away, the eggs
you were supposed to trade for a chocolate rabbit with ears longer
than your hand. I saw that gold egg before Robby Forsgren ever
came near it, but I stood observing it dumbly like I was waiting
for a red light to change, all because Miss Pyke had in plain view
plotted it in the grass right in front of me and even slipped me a
conspiring wink that said, *Here, take it, it's yours*—but I couldn't,
and Robby Forsgren came running and dived for my egg, lum-
bered away, holding it over his head, the coveted chocolate prize
all his, the prize I gave away.

Wonder Woman Hits Theaters, Smashes Patriarchy

I have to admit, I'd been expecting the all-women reboot of *Ghost-busters* to smash the patriarchy once and for all. But disappointedly, it has not, as there are STILL Sleestack lizard people legislating against women's health, women's equality, and women's rights to yoga pants as business casual.

So, when I heard *Wonder Woman* was going to take up Thor's hammer and Hulk Smash the ever-lovin' shit out of this sexist, misogynist universe, can you blame me for being a skoosh-bit dubious? But boy howdy, was I wrong! Since *Wonder Woman*'s release last weekend, we're now living in a post-sexist society. Thank goodness! And right in the nick of time! Color me relieved.

And can you believe there's outrage and protests against women-only screenings? I can't. Wonder Bras are exclusively for women too, but you don't see anyone picketing Victoria's Secret because there's no lingerie for men, no Wonder Bros for dudes. I haven't read any op-eds about *the menz* complaining about women-only bathrooms or women-only prayer groups or women-only volley-ball. But that's all moot now anyway! Because of *Wonder Woman*, we're living in a post-sexist society! Yay!

I heard that Melania Trump saw a women-only screening of *Wonder Woman*, and now she just can't even. How's that for empowerment? Reportedly, she told Donald to go eff himself. If that's true, we're in for a wild ride—for the better, I'd say. *Of course* Melania is going to demand she fly around in an invisible airplane circling Central Park, and *of course* she will add "truth" lassos and indestructible bracelet cuffs to her fashion collection. Go Melania!

Some women reported that they had a religious experience while watching *Wonder Woman*. I don't mean to minimize anyone else's divine inspiration, but that happens to me whenever I sit on the washing machine during its spin cycle.

Don't get me wrong. I'm 100 percent down with smashing the patriarchy if it means I can stay up all night watching the LIFE-TIME Channel and drinking box wine.

So, what's next? Now that all of womankind's menses days are in synch, infertility is a thing of the past, and sperm is obsolete due to some freakish force of nature that causes women to conceive like leopard sharks or Komodo dragons. Can we elect a woman president already? Can I get my spouse to empty the cat box or remember to buy toilet paper? I know that might seem petty, but it's the little things that matter the most to me. If I could talk about my feelings for once without my partner falling asleep, that'd also be super.

Jame Gumb, Hero and Pioneer of the Fat-Positivity Movement

Activist and author *Robbie Tripp* just threw his hat into the ring for Husband of the Year with a body-positive message dedicated to his wife, lifestyle blogger *Sarah Tripp*. In the sweet note shared to Instagram, Tripp recalls being ridiculed for his attraction to women that don't necessarily ascribe to typical beauty standards.

—E! News, August 2, 2017

I love this girl-thing currently trapped in my basement dungeon, and I just love her great-big fat girl-thing body. As a teenager, I was often teased by the whole town and law enforcement for my covetous obsession to girl-things on the thicker side, ones who had short legs and were curvier and who couldn't run away as fast as those thin girls.

As I became a "man" and realized how much I hated and despised my body, I started to educate myself about feminism and body tissues and how I might combat my own disgusting body tissues by making a skin suit sewn from the hides of chubby girls—preferably size 14 or larger. The media likes to portray bigger girls as undesirable, but really, they make the best skin suits; skinny girls just don't cut it.

For me there is nothing that drowns out the demons screaming inside my head better than this girl-thing trapped in my basement dungeon: thick thighs, big booty, cute little side roll on her voluminous back pelt that I can sew darts into, add a ruffle here and there, maybe some butterfly-shaped buttons, etc. Her shape and size will make the perfect outfit for me for my feature on the cover of *Cosmopolitan*. (Fingers crossed!)

Nothing else is more sexy or confident than me trolloped-up and blasting the stereo to "Goodbye Horses" while masquerading in front of the mirror with my pee-pee tucked in. And this gorgeous girl-thing I have trapped in my dungeon will fill out every inch of the rest of my fun little sewing project. I remind her every day to put the lotion on its skin so I can be the most beautiful one in the room.

Guys, rethink what society has told you that you should desire. Desire me. I'm hot. A real woman is not a porn star or a sewing mannequin or even a living, breathing biologically born female. She's real. She's me in a skin suit made out of a crazy-quilt of lady parts and stitched-together hides I hunted and kidnapped myself, replete with authentic stretch marks and cute little dimples on the booty. That's real.

Girl-things, don't ever fool yourself by thinking you have to fit a certain mold to be loved and appreciated. I'll love you—the bigger the better. There is a knuckle-dragging, foaming-at-the-mouth sociopath out there who is going to celebrate you for exactly who you are, someone who will love your soft, supple pelt so much they'll want to wear it as their own.

Post-Election Message to the 53 Percent

More than half of the white women who voted in the presidential election cast their ballot for Donald J. Trump, according to exit poll data collected by the *New York Times*.

I'm a woman, and I supported Donald J. Trump. Well, if you want to split hairs and get all technical about it, I'm not an actual woman per se but a cryogenic cyborg brought here from the future to destroy all of humanity as we know it.

I'm sure you must be thinking that I've either gone DEFCON 1 or that I've logged in too many hours watching the SCI FI Channel. Well, I assure you, everything's going to be *just fine*. I'm not going to start bending shit with my mind like Eleven from *Stranger Things* or anything wacky like that, silly. I'll start from the beginning. Here, hold my laser GLOCK while I adjust your ankle chains. Ha! Just kidding. Nice and easy.

I come from a dystopian future Earth where virtually no women exist. That's right, you heard me. Sometime early in the twenty-first century, following a critical election between a pantsuits activist and an orangutan, all the women of Earth were rescued by a sympathetic alien race and whisked away in fleets of giant spaceships to the planet Clintonia, which is a cross between the island paradise Themyscira, where Wonder Woman was born, and a women's locker room at Club Med.

For the Earth refugees, living among the Aliens on planet Clintonia was a veritable paradise filled with brunch dates followed by yoga and spinning classes, vision board therapy, mani-pedis, evenings watching reruns of *Oprah* and *Downton Abbey*, and box wine—red, white, AND rosé! But something was just not right. I mean, sure, there were zero restrictions on carbs, and no one had ever heard of gluten intolerance or cellulite. Why, for Pete's sake, I once witnessed my master, Carol, suck down an entire five-layer lemon chocolate cake with butter frosting in under a minute! And not once did she shame herself! Now that's a miracle if you ask me!

You might think the obvious reason for the malcontent amid such splendor was because there were no men around to blame shit on or lift heavy objects, but you'd be wrong. Who needs men when there are cyborgs—thank you very much—but the unease continued. The Earth refugees called for a symposium in which the indeterminable sense of that thing no one could put their finger on was much discussed, and it was finally determined that the LaCroix cisterns were critically low. Mama's got to have her LaCroix! So much for revolution.

So, here we are, back from the future to destroy humanity for its LaCroix. Tilting the election in Trump's favor was just the beginning, just the first step. Now, come with me if you want to live. Just kidding! Take me to your LaCroix CEO.

Committee of Barnyard Swine to Determine Fate for Women's Health

WASHINGTON DC—A din of squealing and grunting was heard coming from a White House conference room last Thursday, when top government leaders met with a group of all-male barnyard swine to discuss the future for women's health care.

"The scene at the conference table reminded me of that famous painting of dogs playing poker, only instead of dogs, it's with pigs, and instead of poker, it's Russian roulette," a White House aide reported.

Members of the "Freedom Caucus," a title that the all-swine committee is calling itself, have little if any understanding of women's health and maternity needs, and some elected officials within the GOP have even voiced that the proposal is "unfair" and that barnyard swine shouldn't be expected to subsidize maternity care.

"Making it a requirement for insurance companies to pony up for birthing babies is unconstitutional," a Freedom Caucus member stated. "I've never birthed no baby before. Heck, I've never even seen a baby, but god forbid, if I ever did find myself in the family way, I'd just deal with it privately and call up Stork Delivery R Us or pay a visit to the cabbage patch—ain't nobody be needing none of them fancy maternity services, no how."

Other Freedom Cauci members robustly grumbled and nodded consent: "Uh-huh. I like them French fried potaters, uh-huh."

House minority leader Nancy Pelosi told reporters that the GOP health care bill would make "being a woman a preexisting condition." To which a Freedom Caucus swine rebutted: "That's just what a woman would say. Sounds like a country and western song—*Being a Woman's a Preexisting Condition*. Wasn't that Patsy Cline?"

Last week House Republican leaders pulled the bill to replace the Affordable Care Act with a new health insurance system. Speaker of the House Paul Ryan explained: "We're going to be living with Obamacare for the foreseeable future. I don't know how long it's going to take us to replace this law."

Next up on the agenda for the Freedom Caucus is a reboot of the children's classic *Free to Be You and Me* to be performed in Branson, Missouri, along with an all-swine cast mash-up of *Glengarry Glen Ross* and *Animal Farm*.

Champion Our Native Sisters! (but Only Selectively and under Certain Conditions)

As Indigenous sisters, we need to pull together and lift each other up, individually and collectively. Be the change you want to see happen; be the Gallagher of feminism—only instead of watermelons, smash the patriarchy! You can make a genuine difference in the world by making your Native sisters a priority. Well, almost everyone. Prioritize everyone except Dani Rae—just say no to that ho bag. Everyone else is fine—promote and celebrate everyone else—but not Dani Rae; she's the worst.

By joining together our sacred feminine energies, we can strengthen our families and our amazing Indigenous communities. Did your Indigenous sister Maylene launch a Kickstarter for a trip to the National Teachers' Convention in the state capital? Donate to it! Repost it on your Facebook page! Or better yet, hit up everyone at the office to chip in! That'd be the right thing to do, the *best* thing to do. Help your sisters out . . . well, everyone except Rhondelle, not that hussy. I'm so over that two-faced tramp. She's so fake she must have been made in China. But everyone else I stand behind 100 percent! Sisters unite! Except Rhondelle, not that succubus.

Indigenous women are the essential ingredient in bettering our planet, and if we stand by one another, providing help and support whenever possible, we can effect positive change that will empower all of the lives around us. Well . . . except for Lacey— she needs to step down. That sea hag puts the *vag* in *savage*. But everyone else, all of our other strong and beautiful Indigenous sisters, stand for them! But not Lacey, she's the absolute ~~stupedist~~ ~~stupidist stupitist~~ stupidest.

And definitely not Shawna—nope, that ho thinks she's all that and a bag of chips. Along with Wanda, she eats live snakes for breakfast. And Vanessa, she has a home-wrecker merit badge from the Skank Scouts. But everyone else, all of the other powerful and beautiful Native sisters—treat them with honor and reverence. Their strength is essential to the continuance of our people.

An Open Letter to White Girls Regarding Pumpkin Spice and Cultural Appropriation

Dear Kennedy, Madison, Scout, Britney, Cassidy, Cheyenne, et al.,

Not to sound like I'm singling anyone out here, but as an Indigenous woman, I feel a skoosh bit territorial, to put it mildly, about the commercial appropriation of pumpkin spice and how each year seems worse than the last. I don't mean to exaggerate, but the soon-to-come pumpkin spice season virtually impales me with dread as I wait for the pumpkin spice hysteria to lay siege upon my otherwise placid, pumpkin spice–free life. I don't intend to pumpkin spice shame any-one, but I'm talking to you, Piper, Lisbeth, and Clementine.

Pumpkins and their kinfolk, squash, have a very spe-cific meaning for Indigenous people. Squash is among the three sisters—corn, beans, and squash—and are specific to several eastern tribes, such as the Haudenosaunee (Iro-quois). I hope you will keep that firmly in mind when you order up your next pumpkin spice latte, McKenzie, or light your candelabra of pumpkin spice scented candles nestled among those inevitable gourds so tastefully arranged on your autumnal table, Aspen.

I hope that when you feel that irresistible urge to impulse-buy those pumpkin spice Oreos or that pump-kin spice Special K or even that pumpkin spice–scented Listerine or feminine hygiene product, Mathilda, you'll stop and take a moment to think about the origins of that pumpkin spice Purina Cat Food you're so casually placing on the checkout counter. I hope that you'll pause and reflect upon how your irresistible urge for Pumpkin Spice Cheerios, Hortense, is part and parcel of the same irresistible urge that brought your ancestors to our shores—that same irresistible urge your ancestors had when they slashed and burned, slayed and pillaged, their way across North America in the name of their One True Lord. And while I don't agree that pumpkin spice scratch 'n' sniff liner paper for your cupboards is a particularly wise or dignified choice for your new apartment, Peyton, I can still appreciate a handful of pumpkin spice Skittles just like the next gal, and I can even appreciate the novelty of motherfucking pumpkin spice Ranch dressing, Vanderbilt. I'm not a complete philistine!

I personally have never had a pumpkin spice latte, and even if you handed one to me, Ariel, and even if I was very cold or very thirsty, Lexus, I doubt that I would drink it. I am troubled by the colonial undercurrents of pumpkin spice, Finnegan, and in an effort to create awareness of pumpkin spice cultural appropriation and to help implement safe place environments, Delaney, there needs to be, at minimum, pumpkin spice–free zones at all coffee shops and restaurants and, preferably, assorted autumnal drinks for women of color. Maybe chai or jalapeno chocolate, Chai, I feel that it's important to decolonize the pumpkin, Porsche, and place limits on the settler mentality's love affair with all things pumpkin spice, Hannah.

Yours Truly,
Tiffany Midge

V

Me,
Cutting
in Front
of All
the People
in All
the Lines
Forever:
"It's Okay,
I Literally
Was Here
First."
#DecolonizedAF

Thousands of Jingle Dress Dancers Magically Appear at Standing Rock Protector Site

During a heated standoff between riot police and peaceful protesters, thousands of jingle dress dancers suddenly appeared in the hills overlooking the Standing Rock protest . . . I mean . . . the water protectors' camps.

"Whoa!" John Counts Enemies shouted upon seeing them coming up over the bluff. "LOOK AT ALL OF THE JINGLE DRESS DANCERS!"

"Li-li-li-li-li-li-li-li-li-ing . . ."

The protesters . . . I mean the protectors, gathered and watched in awe and triumph.

"It's a Christmas miracle!" one of the Rainbow Nation protectors cried.

"It's a blessing," Estelle Keeps the Pipe corrected, giving him side-eye.

Loretta Fast Elk commented, "The last time so many jingle dancers came together like this was . . . at that powwow we had in the gym two weeks ago."

The dancers gathered on the main highway and took to the front lines, dancing about 150 yards away from where roughly nine armored police vehicles remained, behind a wall of concrete barriers.

The appearance of the sacred jingle dress dancers came at a very critical time. On Thursday the Morton County Sheriff's Department arrested 141 people, and at least one bullet had been fired from the front lines. Over 300 police officers in riot gear, eight ATVs, five armored vehicles, two helicopters, and numerous military-grade Humvees showed up north of the newly formed front-line camp just east of Highway 1806. The water protectors were armed with sage and sweetgrass bundles.

To add salt to those wounded by rubber bullets and tear gas, the armed antigovernment protesters, led by Ammon and Ryan Bundy, were acquitted Thursday of federal conspiracy and weapons charges stemming from the takeover of a federally owned wildlife sanctuary in Oregon last winter.

"Justice was not served. There's a double standard when it comes to the law. You can be white and armed with weapons and have no consequences, but there's a different set of rules that apply if you're Native protecting your right to clean water," John Counts Enemy stated.

Additional blows were issued when Secretary Clinton, on the very day of the police takedown, gave the following statement with regards to the Dakota Access Pipeline Project (DAPL) conflict: "All of the parties involved—including the federal government, the pipeline company and contractors, the state of North Dakota, and the tribes—need to find a path forward that serves the broadest public interest. As that happens, it's important that on the ground in North Dakota, everyone respects demonstrators' rights to protest peacefully, and workers' rights to do their jobs safely."

"Man, that blows! And I was going to vote for her too! Not anymore!" Celeste Thunder stated upon hearing Clinton's announcement.

"Yeah. I'm not with her anymore—I'm not with any of them. You know who I'm with? I'm with Standing Rock; I'm with water! Mni Wiconi, Mni Wiconi!" Alberta Diaz stated.

"That was a terrible, terrible day, and our hearts were sick and weak, but when we saw the jingle dress dancers rising at the hill's crest, it gave us hope, and our spirits were lifted," Jonelle Fast Elk stated.

Earlier this week the actor Mark Ruffalo, dubbed "Sacred White Ruffalo" by a columnist for *Indian Country Today*, visited Standing Rock. He was joined by Rev. Jesse Jackson, who planned to stand with Standing Rock, and promised, "If necessary, go to jail with them." Jackson was held up by Morton County Police on his way out of Cannonball but not arrested.

"I'm grateful for the Sacred White Ruffalo and Reverend Jackson. We need help. But those jingle dress dancers, ho! That was something!" Clarence Two Bears stated.

The jingle dress dancers could not be reached for a comment. They appeared momentarily on the highway, danced, lifted the spirits of the people, and then dissolved back over the hills from whence they came. The swish and tinkle of their jingles could be heard from beyond the horizon.

Satire Article Goes Viral on Day of 2016 Presidential Election Results

In November, 2016 I published a satire article for *Indian Country Today* about jingle dress dancers miraculously appearing like a mystical herd of sacred buffalo to bless the water protectors at Standing Rock, and my article went viral, receiving tens of thousands of likes and shares on social media. While this was happening, the world sat on pins and needles awaiting the presidential election results: would it be the orange-headed buffoon with a penchant for sexist, racist vitriol? Or would the returns be in favor of Secretary Clinton? What did my satire article and the election results have in common, aside from both receiving a lot of views and reposts? Well, for one, most of the people who liked and shared my article had not caught onto the fact that it was satire. Even the *New York Times* reporter who contacted me was not aware that my article was satire. I get it—tongue and cheek can be subtle. But I suspect it was more than that.

The majority of the general population is functionally illiterate when it comes to Native Americans and First Nations people. I had written that thousands of jingle dress dancers mystically appeared on the hillsides of the Standing Rock protector camps, and sure, while not completely out of the realm of possibility, the idea of "magically" appearing in the surrounding hills as if teleported there by spaceships is a stretch—I should have written *millions* instead of *thousands*. But even so . . .

"Aho," went the comments section.

"American Native Indians are so spiritual."

"I love Native American Indians. I'm part Cherokee."

"Do you know where I can score some peyote?"

While the world held its breath in collective horror and expectation, monitoring the presidential election results streaming in, I kept watch on my article as it gained more and more likes and shares with each passing hour. The article stats climbed higher and higher, while I watched my good comrades on Facebook expressing their despair against the injustice of the election results rolling in. It reminded me of the Orson Welles broadcast of the radio drama *The War of the Worlds* in 1938. The radio audiences listened for hours in abject terror, believing that the world was crashing down around them and that aliens were taking over the planet. Which if you're against the current administration and believe in equality and justice for all, would describe the experience of the election returns to a tee.

Just as the majority of the population is illiterate with regards to Native culture and grossly misinformed about Indigenous people, the majority of the population is also woefully illiterate when it comes to such things as racism, sexism, and living and supporting an authoritative regime. The hardest to accept was the fact that according to the *New York Times* exit polls data, 53 percent of white women had voted for Trump. I had joked that they weren't women per se but cryogenic cyborgs brought here from the future to destroy all of humanity as we know it. I wonder if that headline would be taken for the gospel truth as well.

I read that cinema attendance was at an all-time high during World War II. I thought of this as I woke to the realization that our lives are becoming more and more a real-time dystopian YA novel. And if the entertainment industry thrived in our depressed and harrowing era of war, back when the actual Hitler rose to power, it occurs to me that artists and creators are critically necessary *now more than ever*. Especially humorists and writers of satire.

I've noticed that humor writing has attracted more interest since the election, for instance, and that there is an uptick of published satire. Clearly, we need it.

Perhaps the thousands of jingle dress dancers appearing like pan-Indian angels of mercy was a fiction that all of those tens of thousands of people who responded to my article needed to hear. Perhaps the dancers represented hope in the midst of so much disillusionment. My takeaway was that people can't discern what is real and what is false, like "fake news," for instance. Like mystic warriors painted on the sides of dream catchers. Or worst, of course, that people seem willfully ignorant with regards to casting their ballots for an administration with no investment in their interests.

I'll keep writing, practicing my mode of resistance and activism. And when the people feel despair, think of the jingle dress dancers—real or imagined—appearing across the landscape. Think of them as a blessing. We need it.

Attack of the Fifty-Foot (Lakota) Woman

In September 2016 a fifty-foot monument bearing the likeness of an unnamed Lakota woman, replete with a blowing-in-the-wind star blanket shawl, was installed upon the banks of the Missouri River in Chamberlain, South Dakota. Her creator titled the giantess sculpture *Dignity*.

At the time of *Dignity*'s launch, if you followed the Missouri river to the north, another launch took place—concussion grenades, water cannons, rubber bullets, dog attacks. A launch of incalculable greed and disregard for life. The No DAPL demonstration and standoff was an event on a scale that the world has never seen, and it sparked universal awareness and attention toward the most critically urgent issue of our time.

Protecting the Water. Mni Wiconi. Water Is Life.

The Dakota Access Pipeline Project is expected to cover 1,172 miles and to connect the Bakken and Three Forks production areas in North Dakota to Patoka, Illinois. The pipeline will enable domestically produced light sweet crude oil to reach major refining markets.

The pipeline cuts straight through ancestral lands sacred to the Standing Rock Nation and threatens its main water supply, the Missouri River, Mni Sose.

Ladonna Bravebull Allard, Standing Rock Sioux tribal preservation officer, owns the northernmost land of the Standing Rock Reservation. The northern border is the Cannon Ball River. The eastern border is the Missouri River. From her land you can see the pipeline corridor.

The land she grew up on tells the history of this river back two thousand years.

When I think of the *Dignity* sculpture and the militarization and stand-offs in the small, otherwise peaceful communities on Standing Rock, where my own mother and grandparents were born—and specifically, when I think of monsters in regards to the Black Snake Prophecy—I can't help but think of the 1958 creature feature *Attack of the Fifty-Foot Woman*.

In the movie a rich socialite encounters an alien life form and is transformed into a giantess, a fifty-foot she-beast. The King Kong–sized woman goes on a rampage after discovering her husband is in a bar with a "no-good floozy." Eight industrial-sized hooks, four lengths of chain, forty gallons of plasma, an elephant syringe, and an electrical fire later, she is finally subdued. The authorities responsible for successfully capturing and bringing her down holler things like *I can't shoot a lady! Wadda ya want me to do, salt her tail?*

In my reveries the *Dignity* sculpture breaks from her foundation, secures the blue star quilt firmly around her shoulders, and follows the Missouri River north to Cannonball, up to the Oceti Sakowin—Seven Council Fires—straight into the heart of things, and gets to work killing the black snake.

In my reveries the authorities do not succeed in bringing her down—*eight industrial-sized hooks, four lengths of chain, forty gallons of plasma, an elephant syringe, and an electrical fire.*

In my daydreams she is not defeated but victorious and freeze-framed eternally (despite concussion grenades and dog attacks, water cannons and rubber bullets).

The land she grew up on tells the history of this river back two thousand years.

What stories of this river will be told in two thousand more?

Minnesota Art Gallery to Demolish "Indian Uprisings" Exhibit after Caucasian Community Protest

In 2017 the Walker Art Center in Minneapolis installed a controversial outdoor "gallows" sculpture titled *Scaffold*. The large work included design elements of seven different historical U.S. gallows, including one used to hang thirty-eight Dakota Indians in the state in 1862. Due to protests from Native communities in Minneapolis, the museum agreed to dismantle the gallows. Dakota elders oversaw the dismantling and held a ceremonial burning of the wooden timbers.

The Billy Jack Walking Tall Gallery in Minneapolis came under fire last week for its recent exhibit *Indian Uprisings* by Minneapolis artist Vanessa Kills Twice (Dakota). The installation is a piecing together of various historic U.S. "massacres" perpetrated upon white colonists and pioneers by Native Americans in efforts to protect their lands and their lives.

The central piece, *Scalp*, a fifty-foot statue constructed from metals and recycled materials, depicts the 1804 painting *The Death of Jane McCrea*, by John Venderlyn, and is the culprit for most of the outrage by the Minneapolis Caucasian community.

Margaret Duh, an enraged white resident, spoke out on the issue: "What was the gallery thinking? This is an outrage to the memory of my dear ancestors. Someone in the Caucasian community should have been consulted. Any time a colonist is depicted being bludgeoned to death by clubs, or what have you, it ceases being 'art' and becomes 'atrocity porn.' I'm thoroughly disgusted by the lack of sensitivity the gallery has demonstrated."

Other notable art pieces in the exhibit include a depiction of the 1854 "Ward Massacre" (eighteen members of the Alexander Ward party were killed by Shoshone Indians while traveling on the Oregon Trail) and 1863 Pontiac's Rebellion (Great Lakes, Illinois, and Ohio tribes attacked British forts and settlements; hundreds of colonists were killed).

Gallery docent Clyde Monroe stated: "Some white folks were upset that the 'Whitman Massacre' was installed right next to a playground sculpture of Mickey Mouse and Friends—they felt it was disrespectful to the Whitmans and the missionaries who perished at the hands of Cayuse and Umatilla protectors. I admit it's a pretty gruesome portrayal, but hey, it attracts media attention and keeps our doors open. And it isn't as if the gallery has created permanent installations of church missions for tourism and required construction paper gallows dioramas as part of the public school curriculum. Oh, wait . . . um, never mind!"

Due to the public outcry of community Caucasians, the gallery's director, Wren Ross, will override all suggestions toward facilitating a community gathering to discuss the exhibit and its possible dismantling and, instead, indicated that plans are under way for the exhibit's immediate demolition and removal.

Why I Don't Like "Pussy" Hats

I don't like "pussy" hats for the same reason I don't like the "s word," as in "S Valley" or "S Bay," "S Creek," "S Peak," or "Big S Mountain." Several of these place names have been changed—Isqúulktpe, Umatilla for "throat-slitting place"; Piestewa Peak, named for Lori Ann Piestewa, first known Native American woman to die in combat, first female soldier killed in action in the 2003 Iraq War.

I don't have the luxury or the class status to use appellatives like "pussy" or "nasty." They're not re-claimative terms for someone like me. "Pussy" hats speak liability. "Pussy" hats speak caste system. "Pussy" hats speak privilege. A carefree embrace that lurks without threat.

"Pussy" hats are not transgressive. "Pussy" hats are an emblem, a tool of privilege. When my people march and organize, the cops and paramilitary are deployed. At the Women's March in Washington the demonstrators were free from authoritarian presence. I don't enjoy that same carefree, flagrant luxury my white sisters take for granted.

Because I've known the "s word." I've heard it spoken and used like a weapon to belittle, to declare supremacy, to make war. I've seen it tossed out of car windows, on school playgrounds, in work spaces. Sharpened like obsidian, used to flay open, used to humiliate, to disgrace, to bludgeon, used like an ax.

I've seen it used in a thousand different ways. I don't like "pussy" hats for the same reason I don't like the "s word." I don't like the "s word" for the same reason I reject injustice, ongoing colonialism, racial divide, war, and apartheid.

Li-Li-Li-Li-Land,
Standing Rock, the Musical!

Dear Film Executives,

Due to the overwhelming success of the musical film *La La Land*, I would like to pitch an idea that was inspired by the close-but-no-cigar Best Picture. I mean, hey, glitches aside, it practically won the Oscar, am I right? For sure it won the Oscar for most gracious handover.

My film idea takes the raw energy of *La La Land* and mixes it with the most extraordinary social action and environmental justice event of our time—I'm talking about the No Dakota Access Pipeline Action (No DAPL) at Standing Rock.

Here's how it goes: I see drums and lots of singing and dancing. I see heartbeats of many nations. I see Red Pride, healing, journeying, and good medicine. I see persistence and grit, ancestor-fueled strength. I see a people coming up against a fortress of corporate greed . . . a movie of plain, old-fashioned values, a kind of nostalgia if you will, a movie of the proverbial good versus evil. A new kind of frontier adventure film, a reimagined sort of "western" that reaches beyond "cowboys and Indians."

Now sit back, close your eyes, and picture the opening scene . . .

The scene opens to water protectors gathered on the main highway. Traffic is backed up, and drivers sit impatiently at a standstill while armored police vehicles idle behind a wall of concrete barriers. The sheriff's department is busy arresting dozens and dozens of demonstrators, and there are hundreds of police officers standing by in riot gear.

In the distance the sound of helicopters and military-grade Humvees keep watch over the front-line camp just east of the highway. Tension and a sense of danger fill the air. The water protectors, armed with sage and sweetgrass bundles, begin to ululate—LI-LI-LI-LI-LI-LI-LI-LI!

Above the scene a flying drone camera glides, swirls, and pans to the passengers on the highway as they emerge, one by one, from their cars. A man opens his car door, climbs on top of the hood, and begins dancing and singing. Then another passenger nearby does the same; she climbs to the roof of her car and trills, LI-LI-LI-LI-LI-LI-LI-LI! And then another and another. LI-LI-LI-LI-LI-LI-LI-LI!

A victory yell.

A cop breaks from the offense line and grabs the hand of another cop. They climb on top of one of the Humvees and begin joyfully dancing. Soon all the other passengers waiting on the road begin to follow suit until all the previous tension dissolves into song and dance. The people who were being arrested are let go, and all the people join hands in solidarity and unity.

The sound of LI-LI-LI-LI-ing sparks into the air like elegant lightning. A title appears on the screen: *Li-Li-Li-Li-Land, Standing Rock, the Musical!*

Note: The Dakota Access Pipeline protests began in early 2016 in response to the construction of Energy Transfer Partners' Dakota Access Pipeline in the northern United States. The action drew considerable attention and bolstered the national dialogue about environmental justice significantly.

The film La La Land *is a 2016 American musical romantic comedy drama. It was an Oscar contender for the 2017 Academy Awards.*

VI

Merciless
Indian
Savages?
Try
Merciless
Indian
Fabulous!

Redeeming the English Language (Acquisition) Series

When did he first say "Ugh!"
—"What Made the Red Man Red," from Walt Disney's *Peter Pan*

1. Etymology of *Ugh*

From the *Online Etymology Dictionary*, *ugh* is listed as "imitative of the sound of a cough; as an interjection of disgust, recorded from 1837." And from *Wiktionary*: "used to express repugnance, disgust, boredom, annoyance, tiredness, or horror." Such as: *When I saw how the stuff in the larder had gone moldy, all I could think of to say was "Ugh."*

Ugh may also have its origins in an 1872 memoir about a Creek Indian council held in 1825. Michael Johnston Kenan, who assisted U.S. treaty commissioners at Broken Arrow in the Creek Nation, remembered: "I was particularly surprised by the simultaneous—& clearly, expressed responses or guttural *ugh*'s, of the entire Council—This appeared to be the word of assent or approval that every member uttered, as the speakers rounded or clinched as it were, their statements or inferences—it was as much as 'yes'—'that's so,' or their equivalent meaning."

But it was not until the very popular frontier adventure stories of James Fenimore Cooper that *ugh* was successfully injected into the mainstream vernacular in relationship to all things *American Indian.*

Uncivilized.

Grunting.

Heathen.

1.2 LANGUAGE ACQUISITION

As a small child, I rarely spoke. I didn't have to. My older sister did all the talking for me. When adults asked, "What is your name?" my sister answered, "Her name is Tiffany." I was a ventriloquist's dummy to my big sister's act. I broadcasted my thoughts through a telepathic wave we inexplicably shared, and she, the willing conduit, became the vehicle for my every toddler whim. I had no need for articulation because I didn't *have* to. I probably owe a lot to my sister. It was her enabling of my chronic speechlessness, her Groucho to my Harpo, her yin to my yang, that contributed to my preference for writing—a silent activity—over speaking. She was the mystical channeler, my personal J. Z. Knight, open and receptive to the three-year-old entity I unleashed at her disposal. I was the putty, and she was the hand, and if it was not for her, I may have ended up being a talker instead of a writer, one who runs loudly at the mouth rather than one who purrs quietly at the keyboard. Language came to me in the form of drawing and coloring—reflections of an artistic savant—and gradually this evolved into writing. "Ugh" could easily have been my first utterance. But it could just as easily have been _____.

Universally, across cultures, most every baby's first word is *mama*. In Dakota we say *Ina*.

1.3 PHONOLOGY

I grew up with extra sets of grandparents. This is not so unusual a thing in Native communities. The lineage can be confusing, so

I won't draw you a diagram. Suffice to say, I grew up with three Indian grandmas (Eliza, Ethel, and Charity), and though Eliza tragically died in a car accident before I was born, she remained a constant presence throughout my childhood because her husband, Grandpa Dick, lived with our family. All of my grandparents grew up speaking their tribal languages and retained them into their advanced years. A common occurrence in my house: after dinnertime my mother seated with my grandpa around our yellow Formica table, practicing Dakota.

Linguists who study American Indian English describe the dropping of final voiced obstruents in standard American English. They call this *final devoicing*. It is commonly known among social scientists that the loss of a language is on par with the loss of a species; when a language dies, a piece of humanity dies with it. Indigenous languages are in danger of extinction. Native American languages and culture are inextricably linked because the ideas of a culture are anchored within the language; it is not just a reflection of a culture but *is* the culture. Native cultures have their own set of realities, their own particularities of expression and distinct perceptions of being in the world, and those realities are conveyed through language.

I *still* do not speak my tribal language. Just a smattering of words.

1.4 LITERACY ACQUISITION (EXAMPLE OF DRAMATIC
IRONY OR RUNNING COUNTER TO EXPECTATION)

Spelling bee, 1972. My sister competed against the entire student body at Snoqualmie Valley Elementary School Spelling Bee and won by successfully spelling words like *incendiary, vacuum,* and *hors d'oeuvres.* She went on to compete with the other schools in our district—middle school and high school combined—and won those competitions too: *myrrh, ingenuous, obsequiousness.* When she went on to compete against the winners of the neighboring district, she lost. The word that cost her the competition was *rhythm*. She was a nine-year-old Indian girl with dark skin and braids who out-spelled and out-performed more than two hundred white (WASP) students, many of whom were several grades ahead of her, and she lost to the word *rhythm*.

The drum is the heartbeat of our nation. It remains resistant to English interpretation, to translation—as well it should because how does one translate a heartbeat?

2. The Use of *Ugh* in American Literature

There are numerous references to *ugh* in James Fenimore Cooper's *Last of the Mohicans* (1826). This may well have been the birth of *ugh* as it applies to Native Americans. However, *ugh* was originally scripted as *hugh*, which was later refined by subsequent authors to *ugh* so as not to confuse readers with the man's name Hugh, which is English in origin and means "bright mind."

From *Last of the Mohicans*:

> "Hugh!" exclaimed Chingachgook, who had been occupied in examining an opening that had been evidently made . . . "I would wager fifty beaver skins against as many flints, that the *Mohicans* and I enter their wigwams within the month!"

> When his son pointed out to the experienced warrior the situation of their dangerous enemy, the usual exclamatory "Hugh!" . . . Hawkeye and the *Mohicans* conversed earnestly together in Delaware for a few moments.

> "Hugh!" exclaimed the young *Mohican*, rising on the extremities of his feet, and gazing intently in his front, frightening away the raven to some other prey, by the sound and the action.

Out to the experienced warrior the situation of their danger-
ous enemy, the usual exclamatory "hugh" burst from his. . . ."

This month 9.1 million television viewers tuned in to NBC's
three-hour-long musical production of *Peter Pan Live* (not to be
confused with Disney's animated version). Due to the offensive
Indian-speak gibberish of the "Ugg-a-Wugg" musical number, a
Chickasaw composer, Jerod Impichchaachaaha' Tate reimagined
the song and renamed it "True Blood Brothers"; the "Ugg-a-
Wugg" chorus was replaced with the Wyandot word OWA,HE,
meaning "come here."

While this redo of an inflammatory musical number might
appear to represent some nod toward progress, it more accurately
conveys a kind of compromise. What might seem an effort toward
greater cultural sensitivity to me smacks of something more like
a bargain. As in, *We'll revise the guttural Injun-speak just so long as*
we can still dehumanize actual Native peoples by presenting these
antiquated, stereotypical, racist representations. To my mind, the
costumes, choreography, and staging were as offensive as before,
despite the new song composition.

3. Stages of Language Development (PEPSI)

Level 1. Preproduction Stage (Silent Period):
Minimal Comprehension, No Verbal Production

I keep a photograph of what I believe is my grandmother Eliza,
taken during her boarding school days. In the photo are eight little
Indian girls and eight little Indian boys posing on a shady lawn
beneath the branches of a large tree. The little boys are attired like
George Washington: white wigs, ruffled blouses, cummerbunds,
and breeches, while the girls are posed as elegant debutants replete
with flowery lace and wigs. The children are linking their arms

together in a uniformed sequence as if curtsying before a waltz or cakewalk. Is it strange that the faces of the children in this photograph are downcast? Of course, most photos taken during the 1920s appear this way, except the context forces one to interpret it in a different, more loaded way. It was common to shear children's hair, forbid traditional clothing and customs, and punish children severely for speaking their tribal language. To speak one's own language was an obstacle for acculturation—although I imagine the children must have cried in their beds after the lights were turned out, whispering *Mama* in their tribal language.

Level 2. Early Production Stage: Limited Comprehension;
One- or Two-Word Response
In the sixth grade I rejected the principals of "liberty" and "individualism" by becoming a conscientious objector. Our three classrooms consisted of seventy-five children, all white with the exception of one black boy, a Mexican boy, and me. We weren't exactly a melting pot. Our three teachers brainstormed a self-esteem program and titled it "Especially Special People." The incentive-designed program listed specific criteria for membership, such as extending good deeds, cleaning blackboards, and turning in extra credit assignments. Once a potential "ESP" completed the checklist—much like earning merit badges—they were celebrated in an awards ceremony, given their diploma, and assigned a bright-red ESP button to wear. Probably the best privilege of being an ESP was entry into an elite organization with exclusive benefits such as being allowed to chew gum, purchasing soda from the teacher's lounge, and having extended recesses. For several months I repeatedly resisted becoming *just another* ESP. Every student in our three classrooms, one by one, met the criteria and were indoctrinated and rewarded as Especially Special People—all of the seventy-five children except for two: me

and the Mexican boy, Ricky. On the last day of class, before we were let out for summer break, all of the students left the school grounds and went to a nearby park, where they were treated to an extravagant picnic replete with games, activities, hot dogs, and ice cream. One of the teachers was forced to stay behind in the hot, stuffy classroom with just Ricky and me, as we sat quietly at our desks for the rest of the afternoon.

Level 3. Speech Emergence Stage: Increased Comprehension; Simple Sentences; Some Errors in Speech

Christmas 1971: Her name was Tamu (Swahili for "sweet"), and I had picked her out of the toy section of the Sears catalog. What I did know is that when I pulled her talking string, she spoke the phrases:

- My name is Tamu.
- Cool it, baby.
- Do you like my dress?
- Sock it to me.
- I'm sleepy.
- Can you dig it?
- Let's play house.
- I love you.
- *Tamu* means "sweet."
- I'm hungry.
- I'm proud, like you.

But what I didn't know were Tamu's origins. She was created by Shindana Toys, a division of a company called Operation Bootstrap, Inc., founded as part of a set of initiatives in South-Central Los Angeles in 1968 following the 1965 Watts Riots. A goal of the company was to raise black consciousness and improve self-image. I pulled on Tamu's talking string with such frequency that I ended up breaking her and she never spoke again. Later that year my mother unearthed her old "talking" baby doll. Suzy had a cracked porcelain head, and most of her original, silken yellow hair had fallen off. My mother told me that Suzy would gurgle and fuss when she was laid down, that Suzy would say *Mama*. But she was very old, a 1940s era doll, and had also become mute with age. These were the only baby dolls I ever wanted, or ever kept, and my grandmother told me this was because I was "ina was'te," a good mother.

Level 4. Intermediate Fluency Stage: Very Good Comprehension;
More Complex Sentences; Complex Errors in Speech
1963. Frank Wing, my sister's biological father, waited in a doctor's office with his young wife, our mother, and received the grim news that complications from his type 1 diabetes was rapidly progressing and that he should not expect to live beyond six months. It was a Friday, November 22, the same day President Kennedy was fatally shot while riding with his wife, Jacqueline, in a presidential motorcade. My mother and Frank heard the tragedy broadcasted on the car radio after the doctor visit. *Where were you when you heard?* Their breath would have expelled in frosty plumes, like smoke, as they waited for the engine to warm. My mother would have reached over with her gloved hand and switched off the radio.

My sister was almost three months old when Frank and my mother were confronted with the prognosis. Yet despite the news that he was terminally ill and despite having gone blind, Frank continued his studies in the Education Department at Northern Montana College. My mother read out loud from his textbooks each evening, going over every lesson, while they drank cups of black coffee at the yellow Formica table.

Fifty Shades of Buckskin

Native American romance novels and historical romance novels have been around for a while, as far back as captivity narratives such as Mary Rowlandson's. The modern version captivity narratives are typically trade paperbacks with brawny, half-breed "braves" posed in various compromising positions with scantily clad white women with fiery-red tresses. Think *Love American (Indian) Style*. Think *Sex and the City Indian*. Think twenty-first-century Fabio, Channing Tatum, or Jason Momoa in a seventeenth-century loincloth. The braves, direct from central casting, appear out of the covers like preferred members of Little Gold's Gym on the Prairie replete with glistening pecs and rippling, savage six-packs. They look like they could lift a buffalo. And that's the whole point, isn't it? Because devotees of "buckskin" romances want to be lifted; they want to be carried away! And the girth of the brave's . . . um . . . arms is in direct proportion to the (sizzling) force of the narrative. Or so the covers lead us to believe.

The biggest offender of buckskin style romances are the *Savage* historical novels. The series sells worldwide to millions of fans. The book titles include *Savage Heat, Savage Moon, Savage Wonder, Savage Passions, Savage Spirit, Savage Thunder, Savage Hawk, Savage Illusion, Savage Stomach Indigestion, Much?* Well, you get the point. The author has cornered the market, and if it has *savage* in the title, you know who probably wrote it.

Just for fun, I'll pick up one of these books and skim to a particularly steamy scene and mentally replace the sexually objectified "half-breed" romantic hero with that of a palomino stallion. Because that is the way the authors of these books draw their characters, as wild, "savage" beasts. If the genre's readers ever talked to an actual Native person or set foot in any actual Native community, they might be in for a shock.

So, to help reconcile this offense, and help clear up any malignant distortions, I decided to create some contemporary literary scenes straight from the annals of what I imagine to be a more realistic portrayal—albeit fictional version—of Native American romance.

Skinny Jeans and All

Janelle Jon-Jon Fast Elk got up off the couch and drove to the mall to buy light bulbs and a rotisserie chicken. But dark storms were brewing. Her check card wouldn't work. So she tried calling the bank, but her cell phone had run out of minutes! In a cruel twist of fate she had to drive home again! But her car stalled out in the middle of an intersection! A harrowing saga replete with breathtaking vistas and romantic intrigue. Along the way Janelle meets a tall, ashen-haired stranger wearing suspenders and an ironic mustache. She's been warned by elders not to date hipsters, but the tall stranger's mischievous eyes lure her heart to him—skinny jeans and all.

Fry Bread Grease

Danny's all bad boy, a citified, urban skin who's into hip hop and always organizing Free Leonard Peltier rallies. But that all changed when the super-tradish, old-school Sandy came into his life! Sandy can talk to coyotes like Dr. Doolittle, so sweet she could rot your teeth just being in the same room. She runs the elder program on the rez. Can their love survive?

Stands-with-a-Stiffy

As long as Petunia Snodgrass can remember, she's been haunted by unbidden images of a Comanche warrior called Stands-with-a-Stiffy. One fateful day her curiosity about the strange dream is forever quenched. Who would have thought she'd discover the reincarnation of her one true love at the nearby tribal casino? And who would ever have imagined that her forevermore love would be in the form of a slot machines assistant manager who drove a Celica hatchback!

Good Medicine

Ever since Nancy Medicine Deer could remember, she always wanted to be a registered nurse. But was that enough? Why stop there when she could be an MD? But how would she ever pay for tuition and cover her bills at the same time? The answer to her dilemma soon arrives in the form of the beguiling modern-day snake oil salesman, Damien Thorne, who recruits naive Nancy into his Native American Spiritual Retreat Seminars. For a thousand dollars participants are given sacred instructions for cleansing. Nancy suspects something strange when Damien introduces her to the first rite, which involves a brush, ammonia, and the dashing Damien's kitchen floor.

Crow Fair Sunrise

It is fiery-red-tressed Madison Monroe's first visit to the infamous Crow Fair in Indian Country, and she can scarcely believe her emerald-green eyes. She mistakenly assumed there would be carnival rides and is initially disappointed, but she soon discovers a different and better kind of ride she never would have anticipated. When raven-haired Napoleon Pretty Bird saunters up to Madison and roguishly inquires if she would like to wojapi his pemmican, what else can a girl do? When in Rome!

Per Caps in Paradise

"It's so hard to find a decent parfleche bag to match my Jeep Wrangler," photojournalist Trioux Lautrec laments. "A girl's got to hunt and gather, after all." Meet Trioux, the sassy incarnation of Sacagawea and Calamity Jane. Meet her trusty sidekick, Sunka Was'te, her loyal, three-legged German shepherd. While scouting for pictorials on the Fort Bantz Reservation, Trioux encounters the dazzling Zola fancy-dancing to a lame remix of "Purple Rain" at the local watering hole. It's not long before the two girls start inventing some dance steps all their own, with surprising and sizzling results!

Dances with Werewolves

Legends prevail darkly along the Wishawah Coast Indian Reservation, and the locals warn visitors against traversing the forest and beaches after dark, especially during nights of the full moon. So, when proud Indian maiden Abigail House's defiant nature sets into motion a series of supernatural events, the inhabitants of Wishawah and all of the future are threatened. That is, unless the reclusive Wolf Clan, led by the mysterious Julian Ross, can lay claim to Abigail's soul before the terrifying spirits are released.

Moccasin Telegraph

Thelma Two-Moccasins thought her life held no more surprises until her grandson Tiger hooked up a computer and Wi-Fi in her small apartment at the Tribal Assisted Living Center. Soon she was surfing the web like a boss. And when a kindly instant message popped up with the screen name YogiBare4U, Thelma's fate was about to turn a sharp corner. But would she accept destiny's offer?

Conversations with My Lakota Mom

In observance of Mother's Day, I'd like to share a personal anecdote about my mom: *Spring had arrived, the sun was heating things up, and it was time to plant the garden. My mother wanted to put in yellow beans, a type of bean she'd never gardened before. She carefully read the planting instructions, her eyeglasses balanced at the end of her nose. "Only plant in full, direct sunlight." She looked up from the seed packet, surveyed the sky, the incoming clouds; it was nearing sunset, and soon it would be dusk. So my mother put away the packet of seeds to plant for the next day.*

This story illustrates my mother's, shall we say, decidedly *unique* personality in a way that no other story can quite compare. But I'll try to top it with the following collection of interactions between a forty-something daughter and her seventyish Lakota mom titled "Conversations with My Lakota Mom," which represents a kind of amalgamation of some Native moms I've been lucky enough to have in my life.

Conversations with My Lakota Mom, No. 1

—For my seventieth birthday I want to hire them sexy Chippewa dancers to come entertain at my party.
—Don't you mean the *Chippendale* Dancers?
—No, not the chipmunks!

Conversations with My Lakota Mom, No. 2

—Where're we going?
—I'm taking you to lunch—buckle your seat belt.
—Where?

—Old Country Buffet.

—*Harrumph.*

—What's wrong?

—You're taking me to Costco's for the free samples again.

—No. I'm not!

—Yes, you are, that's where you took me last time. And then you tried to tell me the hot dog condiments was a salad bar.

—Fine. You're on to me. But you like the samples. They have crescent rolls! It's cheap, and I'm in a hurry.

—You should buy toilet paper while we're there.

—Okay.

—And pretzels.

—Really?

—And a honey baked ham.

—Um.

—See? Taking me to Old Country Buffet would be cheaper.

Conversations with My Lakota Mom, No. 3

—Can you drive me to the tribal clinic next week? I have a woman appointment.

—Yeah. I can.

—I have a lady time appointment.

—Yeah, okay . . .

—That's my vagina doctor . . .

—Right, got that.

—I have to show that doctor my business down there . . .

—Um, TMI, Mom!

—Sigh.

—What?

—Sigh.

—Okay, what?

—They stopped asking me certain questions.

—Like what?

—Like when was the last time Scarlett came home to Tara.

—Mom!

—(*Giggles*) And they always ask me if I feel safe at home.

—Oh?

—Yes, they want to know if you're beating me. They say, Lorraine, is your daughter beating you?

—Tell them I'm thinking about it.

—Elder abuse!

Conversations with My Lakota Mom, No. 4

(*Getting ready for a memorial service*)

—When I make the journey play Neil Diamond at my funeral. Play *Girl, You'll Be a Woman Soon*. Your dad and me conceived you with that song.

—Um. Okay, Mom.

—It's a good song. If you played that more often, I might have more grandchildren.

—I'll get right on that.

—Are theme funerals a thing? I'd like pony rides, corn dogs ... but don't bury me! Just let people throw balls at a dunk tank target to sink my body into the abyss.

—Um ...

Conversations with my Lakota Mom, No. 5

—I like that one guy ... what's his name? That Ind'n actor ...

—Wes Studi?

—No, that other one.

—Gary Farmer?

—Uh, no, what's his name ...

—Adam Beach?

—No. He was in *Dances with Wolves*. He married that white woman with the big hair, the one who looked like she just came from Vidal Sassoon.

—What? No.

—He's so handsome!

—Um.

—Your dad was handsome like that Ind'n Dances with Wolves.

—Um, that's Kevin Costner, Mom. He's NOT Indian.

—Well he played one on TV.

—You didn't just say that!

—(*Grinning*) I did. I like seeing you get all riled up.

Conversations with my Lakota Mom, No. 6

—I walked three miles on the treadmill yesterday.

—Wow, Mom! Good for you!

—Yes. I was watching this TV show, it gave me pep.

—Yeah? What were you watching? NASCAR?

—No. What's NASCAR?

—Never mind. What were you watching?

—It was this show about Indians running all of these buffalo off a cliff.

—Oh? I saw that before. That's *Into the West*.

—Yeah. *Into the West*. I figured I better get the lead out. All our ancestors running alongside buffalo, on horseback, beneath a hot plains sun.

—Yeah?

—They humbled me, so I walked extra to honor them. I hope the grandfathers are smiling.

—That's good. Next time you can work out on the rowing machine and pretend you're Sacagawea mapping a trail to the Pacific.

—Yeah. I'll be Sacagawea, getting my groove back. They can put me working out on the rowing machine on the twenty-dollar bill.

Feast Smudge Snag

Feast Smudge Snag

You've read the book *Eat Pray Love*, and you've seen the movie starring Julia Roberts. Well, hold onto your fry bread because here's the Lakota version, *Feast Smudge Snag*. Synopsis: In her early thirties Colleen Campbell had everything a modern Indigenous woman could hope for—four great kids, a condo, a successful Etsy shop—but instead of feeling fulfilled, she was overcome by anxieties and confusion. This wise and transformative book is the story of how she overcame her worries and set out to reclaim the traditional aspects of her culture and renew a sense of balance back into her life. Not by visiting Italy, India, or Bali but by burning some sweetgrass and looking right in her own backyard.

How Sacagawea Got Her Groove Back

Go west, they said; it'll be fine, they said. Little did our iconic heroine know she'd be stuck for months on end, forging a trail with thirty unruly laborers and a baby strapped to her back. Little did she realize that after enduring illness, flash floods, temperature extremes, food shortages, and mosquito swarms, all that she'd receive in compensation was a commemorative coin just shy of two hundred years too late. What's an Indian guide to do? Go to Jamaica, man, sip mimosas on the beach, and indulge in an island fling with a much younger man.

Bead by Bead

In 1995 the how-to instructional manual for writers *Bird by Bird* made its stunning debut. But have you ever heard of the Indigenous version, *Bead by Bead*? As any good bead artist knows, when crafting earrings, a belt buckle, or a bolo tie, you just got to be patient and take it bead by bead. *Bead by Bead: Instructions for Indigenous Writing* applies the same principles of the craft of beading to the craft of writing. Whether you're writing the Great American (Indian) Novel, a blog post, or just a postcard, you're only going to achieve the end result by keeping your focus on the small details and taking it one bead, or one word, at a time.

The Casinos of Madison County

For anyone who has ever experienced the heartache of The-Snag-Who-Got-Away, *The Casinos of Madison County* is the book for you. Synopsis: It's lonely on the plains, and housewife and mother Fran Lone Elk's marriage has grown stale and humdrum over the years. Enter the tall, dark, and handsome *National Geographic* photographer who by chance stops by her isolated HUD house, lost and looking for directions to the casino. With Fran's husband and children away, Fran climbs into the mysterious photographer's truck and directs him to the casino and then the next casino and the next. Over the next four days—because four is a sacred number—Fran's loneliness transforms into a mad, passionate love affair . . . with slot machines.

The Color Turquoise

Alice Walker's *The Color Purple*, winner of the 1983 Pulitzer Prize, captured many a reader's heart throughout the world. Here's the Indigenous version we'd like to see, called *The Color Turquoise*. Meet our heroine, a girl named Turquoise, a woebegone woman who, with grit and determination, overcomes her heartbreaking circumstances with a little help from her sisters and friends. Not everyone is lucky enough to have a champion jingle dress dancer—Sugar Everybody Talks About—as a BFF, but there's some special kind of chemistry that happens whenever the two girls get together. Can this be the key to unlocking Turquoise's dreams?

A Confederacy of Dunces with Wolves

While bearing striking similarities to the cult classic novel *A Confederacy of Dunces* written by John Kennedy Toole, published posthumously and winning a Pulitzer Prize, *A Confederacy of Dunces with Wolves*, however, did not receive the same literary success. Some critics pointed out that had *A Confederacy of Dunces with Wolves* used New Orleans as its setting, instead of the plains of Nebraska, it might have been a best seller—or at the very least made into an Academy Award–winning film.

Harry Pottahontas

Harry Pottahontas is a delightful series of chapter books about a magical Native American boy who rides buffalo and talks to unicorns. Perhaps you've heard of it? If not, then certainly you've heard of its doppelgänger series, *Harry Potter*, by J. K. Rowling? The central takeaway: being that so many white people believe Indians practice magic, you'd think they'd try and be nicer to us.

Are You There, Tunkasila? It's Me, Margaret, Looks Back

Growing up can be a hard road, and with so many bodily changes happening, life can sometimes feel overwhelming and even scary. *Are You There, Tunkasila? It's Me, Margaret, Looks Back* helps to negotiate those trails toward womanhood and will provide solace for any young girl who might feel alone and is looking for her path. Of course, a young Native girl can always look for guidance within her Tiyóspaye, but it's comforting to know that a good book is always within reach.

Eight Types of Native Moms

What type of mom raised you? While the definitions of motherhood vary from culture to culture and region from region, mothering styles can be as different as individual personalities. Everyone will bring their own set of values to the table, but here are eight kinds of Native moms you might be familiar with. Now sit up straight and eat your vegetables.

The Everybody's-Mom Mom: This is the mom who takes in everybody's else's kids and calls them her own. The mom whose personal adage is "There's more enough to go around" and "The more the merrier." If you grew up thinking that your bed was a sleeping bag on the floor next to six other kids—or eight or eleven or twenty—who you thought were your siblings, you might be the child of an Everybody's-Mom Mom.

The Hawk Mom: Sometimes referred to as a helicopter mom, or helicopter parent, the Hawk Mom never lets you out of her sight, and if for one fleetingly carefree moment you fell out of her bionic-strength range of sight, she would swoop down and scoop you up into her proverbial wingspan and rush you to "safety." It's a wonder you ever learned how to walk, let alone crawl, by yourself. If you never learned to tie your shoes and still only buy Velcro, you might have been brought up by a Hawk Mom.

The Cougar Mom: No, not that kind of "cougar." The Cougar Mom is akin to the Tiger Mom, which the author Amy Chua made famous with her best-selling book *Battle Hymn of the Tiger Mother*. The Cougar Mom runs a ship so tight that she makes yoga pants seem blousy. This mom doesn't just put the *line* in *discipline*, but she invented the line, as in: Don't you dare think to cross it if you know what's good for you!

Basketball Mom: The Basketball Mom is close cousins with the Soccer Mom. If your mom was a Basketball Mom, chances are you know your way around a basketball court. This mom logged in hours and hours courtside and hundreds of miles annually driving you from game to game. Her enthusiasm and team spirit are unmatched to the point that by the end of every season, you wondered if aliens stole her body and replaced her with Basketball Mom, the impostor who hadn't taken off the team's jersey except to shower, and even then, you couldn't be sure. Added benefit: Basketball Mom brought the best snacks during halftime.

Powwow Mom: In other circles she is known as Pageant Mom or Stage Mother. Did you hear about the Powwow Mom who fed her daughter jumping beans so her daughter would have more pep in her step when she danced jingle dress? No? Well, that's because it's a made-up story. Powwow Mom is another version of Basketball Mom, only without the free throws. She's the mom who'll stay up all night working on your dance regalia tirelessly and without complaint, who will bead your crown, cuffs, or cape until her fingers bleed. You're actually pretty lucky—she'll probably be the biggest supporter you'll ever have in your life, so enjoy it while you can.

Tribal Council Mom: If your mom was on Tribal Council, everybody thought you received special entitlements and kickbacks. And chances are you probably did. But the drawback was that if you ever did anything wrong, like act out in class or neglect to turn in your homework, she would be the first one to hear about it, and as a result, you were a model student. Having a mom on Tribal Council was like having a parent who was your school principal or being the pastor's kid. Although it wasn't so bad, since most councils rotate out members every few years.

Super-tradish Mom: If you were carted around in a cradleboard until age five, your mom might have been super-tradish. If your mom packed your lunchbox exclusively with dried huckleberries and buffalo jerky, when everyone got bologna sandwiches and Twinkies, she might have been a Super-tradish Mom. If you were sent to school wearing moccasins or ribbon shirts and everyone else wore sports jerseys and Jordans, your mom might have been super-tradish.

Chill Mom: Chill Mom is basically the equivalent to what's referred to as a free-range parent. Chill Mom is laid-back and figures that if it's something important, then you'll eventually figure it out for yourself. Chill Mom thinks that if you're still alive by the end of the day, then she's done her job. It isn't that Chill Mom is negligent so much as she is hands-off and believes that she's not doing you any favors by over-supervising. The opposite of Hawk Mom, Chill Mom expects that you know what you're doing. If you packed your own lunches and walked yourself to school, you likely had a Chill Mom.

VII

"Shill the Pretendian, Unfav the Genuine"
Is the 2018 Remix of "Kill the Indian, Save the Man"

Red like Me

I Knew Rachel Dolezal Back When She Was Indigenous

In 2015 the media exploded with coverage about a woman who claimed she was African American. Her name is Rachel Dolezal, and her name has since become synonymous with racial scandal and identity confusion. While the world watched Dolezal's tall tales unfold and while her web of lies and deception grew more and more tangled with each passing (news) day, I inwardly sighed and tried to impress upon my social circle, those IRL and on social media, "This is nothing new for us Natives." And to borrow an apropos lyric from Shania Twain, a white pop star from the nineties whose own identity was not without its share of complications (her stepfather was Ojibway): "That don't impress me much."

Well, wouldn't you know it, like the Eveready Energizer Bunny, Dolezal is back in the news again, giving interviews and promoting her new book, so I thought this would be an opportunity to share my riveting story about the time I personally met Rachel Dolezal—back when she used to be Indigenous! Yes, that's right, Rachel Dolezal used to be Native American! An obscure fact only I and a handful of people are privy to. Today I'm breaking my silence.

It happened over a decade ago, when I was writing an investigative think piece in response to pretendianism. Critical questions I wished to explore were: *Who are these pretendian persons? Where did they come from? Why are they here? Why did that one steal my job? What's with all the turquoise accessorizing and black shoe polish?* I needed some answers. Interestingly enough, since pretendians make up somewhere in the ballpark of 54 percent of the population in the United States (I'm no statistician, but that's a huge percentage!), I didn't have to journey far for answers. Turned out, it wasn't the epic quest I'd imagined. I didn't have to team up with Gandalf and my Hobbit friends and traverse through mountains, snow, darkness, forests, rivers, and plains, facing evil and danger at every corner, to destroy the One Ring in the hopes of ending the Dark Lords reign. But, boy howdy, it was close!

I called up a friend of a friend of this one guy who had a cousin who knew a pretendian, and the pretendian graciously agreed to meet me at a nearby tea shop for an interview. (Speaking of a friend of a friend, I assumed pretendians fit into the rubric of six degrees of separation, except they actually don't—more like two degrees of separation; again, I'm no statistician.)

Upon entering the tea shop—aptly called Animal Spirit Tea Shop—I noted the ambient tones of the so-called Native American flute wafting from the speakers, the sweet aroma of sage and patchouli, patrons lounging on large cushions, some quietly talking, some blissfully nodding off. I had the odd sensation of being inside an opium den, circa 1920, San Francisco. Had I just blood quantum leaped?

The pretendian subject's name was Faith Eagle Nebula, and yep, that's right, known today as Rachel Dolezal! Ms. Dolezal—or rather, Ms. Eagle Nebula—indicated in her email that she had long black hair (a weave, it turns out) and that she would be wearing a peasant skirt and Birkenstocks, a description that fit 99 percent of the patrons in the tea shop, which forced me to break out my specialized Indian radar to locate her. When that didn't work, fortunately, the Grandfathers stepped in and brought Faith Eagle Nebula to me; Faith tapped me on the shoulder and introduced herself. Pure magic!

Faith Eagle Nebula was adorned in her pretendian regalia just as she described, her peasant skirt pooling onto the floor and dragging behind her like a bridal train. "I'm Faith," she said, her eyes sparkling, her cheeks rosy as a postcard sunset. She smelled strongly of spices and wind chimes tinkling in the breeze—that is, if wind chimes even had a particular smell. Very strange. She led me to a cozy nest of pillows, and we laid down to begin the interview. From my lounging position I scanned the ceiling, taking note that it was plastered with figures from the zodiac. Faith offered to massage my back, but I managed politely to decline.

My first question to Rachel Dolezal—aka Ms. Eagle Nebula—was how she got her name. I'm sure it was impolite of me to ask, but any investigative journalist worth her salt has to ask the hardline questions. She responded by gesturing dramatically and then said that her name came to her in a dream. Elaborating further, she said that like many other pretendians, she'd carried other names throughout her life too. Her first pretendian name was Roadkill Squirrel, a name that she said she couldn't talk about because it was too upsetting. Other pretendian names she'd carried in previous lifetimes included Dances thru Meadows Womyn, Frolics on Freeways, Laughs with Salad, and Stands with Handcuffs—the last one, she explained, was given to her during her political activism years. She asked me my own pretendian name, and I humored her and said it was Dances through Drive-thrus. She nodded and mumbled, "Aho."

I asked Rachel Dolezal—aka Ms. Eagle Nebula—about her ethnicity, her specific tribal affiliation, and who her relatives were. Ms. Eagle Nebula responded quickly by excusing herself to get us another pot of yerba mate. It was almost as if she was avoiding my question! She was gone for what seemed an eternity, and when she came back to our soft nest of colorful cushions, she was without the pot of yerba maté but said she'd like to smudge me. I reluctantly agreed, and while she checked her iPhone for sacred winds and good medicine, I crossed my fingers behind my back to ward off whatever strange spell she might be putting on me. You can never be too careful.

When I resumed my interview, asking again about her ethnicity, tribe, and relatives, she said that whenever she filled out the ethnicity sections of job, grant, or health applications, she always checked the "it's complicated" box. I told her that wasn't a box but a relationship status on Facebook, and she replied that she was aware of that but that she always added it, as a safeguard. She also said that she writes in "high cheekbones" when applications ask for proof of tribal citizenship, implying that she's from the "High Cheekbone band of the Pretendian Nation." Then Faith made the sign of the cross and said that her spirit animal was the wolf, at which point I threw up in my mouth a little bit.

I asked Rachel Dolezal—aka Ms. Eagle Nebula—whether she was aware that pretendians present a real and present danger to the integrity of Native communities because they usurp authentic Native voices and dilute, cheapen, and perpetuate harmful stereotypes. Ms. Eagle Nebula appeared unfazed by this information and pivoted my questions by announcing that she had received a vision while browsing the Aztec-inspired crop tops at Old Navy. "Those crop tops were amazing! I bought a dozen of them," she said. She went on to recount her lunch the day before at Panda Express. "You know, I used the WHOLE part of the kung pao chicken entrée, even the leftover chopsticks!" Faith removed the chopsticks from the topknot bun in her hair and placed them in my hand. "These are sacred talking sticks," she said.

As if right on cue, the fire alarm sounded, and the tea baristas began ushering people out of the shop. I gathered up my belongings and rushed out, following the stampede of dream catcher earrings, turquoise squash blossom necklaces, and Birkenstocks to safety. Faraway in the distance, I heard fire trucks and emergency vehicles speeding to the scene. What kind of uncanny magic was this?!

Around the corner from the tea shop, I waved goodbye to Rachel Dolezal, aka Faith Eagle Nebula, and offered a shrug, which is the international gesture for *wadda ya gonna do*. She bowed in return, just before being whisked onto the back of a pink unicorn and ferried away into a puff of rainbow cotton candy clouds. On the way back to my office, I ran through a set of lawn sprinklers, hoping that I could shower off the encounter and extinguish the reek of patchouli from my clothes.

While I did not complete the interview, I would like to interview Rachel Dolezal at a later date and once and for all get to the bottom of the perplexing phenomena of pretendian culture—a mystery akin to the Egyptian tombs, the Bermuda Triangle, and the Lost City of Atlantis. Aho.

A List of Alternative Identities to Try for Fun and Profit

Has pretending to be Indigenous ever gotten you down? Is your farce starting to wear a little thin? Do you feel like you're in a slump? Tired of the unending grind of playing make-believe and stealing from Native Americans? If you're feeling unfair backlash from pretending to be Indigenous and your Indian disguises are no longer cutting it, you should try Hoodwink Identities. Here at Hoodwink Identities we realize what a slog it can be to duck and dodge the criticism of others and to find yourself forever on the defensive. It's almost as if you're a bandit on the lam or some garden-variety hooligan evading the popo. We realize how stressful Indigenous identity pirating can be, and that's why here at Hoodwink Identities we offer several fine *alternative* packages for all of your hornswoggling needs.

COYOTE ACME: Coyote is the quintessential huckster and sure to meet all of your flimflam needs. This package is perfect for pretendians of all levels, beginning, intermediate, or advanced. For a limited time only, this package comes with a free all-you-can-eat buffet of bologna-sauce or your choice of anvils, dynamite, and baby grand pianos. Look out for Roadrunner!

RHODODENDRON BUSH: No one would ever suspect the non-descript, guileless rhododendron bush—why, even former communications director Sean Spicer endorses the efficacy of the bush. It's not just for evading the press core anymore! Buy now while limited supplies last. Also comes in azalea, rose, and hydrangea.

WINDIGO: If you can't win them over with your charm, try scaring them into submission. Works better than a Stephen King scary clown hiding in the storm drain every time! So terrifying you'll have them crapping their pants!

JUSTIN TRUDEAU: Our highest-selling package, as popular in the United States as in Canada. While it isn't always easy to convince people that you're the prime minister of Canada, you'll certainly have fun trying. Package comes with free *Justin Trudeau Is My Spirit Animal* T-shirt and trucker cap.

THE ELEMENTARY SCHOOL LUNCH LADY: Do you enjoy the laughter of children? Then this package is for you! It comes with a free hot lunch, hair net, and plastic apron. No one knows what happens to the lunch lady after school meals are served. Does she live in the walk-in freezer? Is she a member of the foreign legion? The lunch lady is as mysterious as the mystery meat served on Taco Tuesdays.

A REAL-LIVE FUCKING GRIZZLY BEAR: Go ahead, be daring, be bold, be king of the fucking forest, or don a top hat and a pair of tap shoes and dance at the Mall of America. So what if you're just wearing last year's marked-down Chewbacca costume from Halloween Discount Xpress—people believe just about anything these days. Tell them you're a fucking griz, they'll buy into it. They're like Mikey; they'll eat anything.

HISTORICAL RACIST PUBLIC STATUE: This package is perfect for blending in at any occasion and provides the ideal backdrop for eavesdropping on private conversations, loitering, or party and event crashing. You'll rival the chocolate fondue and champagne fountain, and this disguise is a big hit with the kids and pigeons. Exercise caution when using; public statues are prone to toppling and spontaneously combusting. We're currently offering a special on our Mount Rushmore package.

I Have White Bread Privilege

I love sandwiches, all kinds, and anyone who knows me knows that I love me a sammich! But what people don't know about me, and something that is deeply uncomfortable to admit, is that ... I prefer white bread.

Now that might not be a very politically correct thing to say, and I appreciate how that might be wrongly taken, and yeah, I know all about white bread's nutritional content or lack thereof and that gluten is just plain hazardous for many people. Spare me the lectures—I know all about white bread, okay?

But the gist is, I have white bread privilege.

It started sometime around elementary school, when all of the other kids' moms packed their sandwiches for them, and at lunchtime they opened their *My Little Pony, Dukes of Hazard,* and *Gremlins* lunch boxes and pulled out tuna fish and deviled ham sandwiches made out of ... yep, you guessed it, Wonder Bread. If you didn't have a bologna sandwich made out of Wonder Bread, it made you a freak, it made you pathetic, it made you mos def uncool. I always insisted on white bread, and it has stuck with me throughout my life, and while I understand that this preference is problematic in today's anti–white bread, anti-gluten, and anti–processed food climate, what can I say? Old habits die hard.

Some of my friends will ask me, why should you apologize for your white bread preference? You can't help liking what you like—I mean, it isn't as horrible as all that, is it? It isn't as if you're drowning a sack of puppies or drawing comparisons between skin tones to different kinds of foods—you know like "chocolate skin" or "caramel-russet-gravy-colored skin." You just have a preference. And you happen to believe that white bread simply is . . . well, better than dark bread.

If you must know, I haven't come to this reconciliation without a struggle. See, my preference for white bread and overcoming my guilt for preferring white bread have not come without their share of a dark-night-of-the-soul kind of battle. I mean, I've really agonized over this! It isn't that I think dark bread is bad, I understand that many people prefer dark bread not only because it's healthier but also because they find it more to their tastes, and for those folks I say, that's okay. I just happen to prefer white bread.

One of my friends informed me that because I identify as an Indigenous person, I shouldn't prefer white bread because white flour is an evil, colonialist, settler ingredient. And evil, colonialist, settler foods have wreaked havoc on the health of Native populations—health problems like diabetes. While I understand all too well the statistics and the health issues, I still prefer white bread.

I am a Native American who has white bread privilege.

The other pressing issue I need to talk about is dark bread passing for white bread. Many of you might be aware of this, and some of you might not. The white bread companies like Wonder Bread try to trick consumers by disguising their white bread to make it look like brown bread. When I first became aware of this, I was all WTH? That's so not cool! For what possible reasons would the companies do that? It is not only confusing, but it totally undermines the authenticity of white bread *and* dark bread. And furthermore, I might be enjoying my white bread sandwich, but how do I know for sure that it's really white bread? Maybe I'm eating dark bread that is passing for white bread? Man, that blows my mind a little. Bread is so complicated. Bread is so fluid a construction.

I don't mean to shanghai the conversation away from the other more pressing issues; I don't want to come off like a d-bag and make this all about me and my white bread privilege! Because I totes get that there's a lot of people who don't even have a choice as to what bread they like best because there's, like, no bread to be had! And that blows. Like, I get it. But if you don't mind, I'm talking about me right now.

And I didn't want to bring this up, but I may as well put it out there—tortillas do the same thing. Some tortillas at the grocery store are not only white and brown but also green! And orange! And yellow! Like a rainbow, these tortillas. Like a Skittles commercial, these tortillas.

Thanks. It feels good to get this off my chest—my unbearable white bread–ness of being.

Things Pseudo-Native Authors Have Claimed to Be but Actually Are Not

With the increasing number of non-Indigenous people claiming Indigenous ancestry—in particular authors such as Joseph Boyden, subject of the most recent controversy, and academic Andrea Smith as well as many other preeminent intellectuals and professional Indian experts—it's critical that we understand the motivations behind these misrepresentations and find reasonable ways to address and resolve these incidents from happening further.

Veronica Faust, PhD and noted ethnologist-entomologist, whose dissertation on pretendian behavioral science from the University of Chicanery offered insights on this epidemic phenomena, suggests: "One way to respond to charlatan controversies and identify instances of ethnic fraud is to look to other species and analyze the ways that they mitigate these kinds of impostor issues. Animals, specifically insect species, have the same instincts for survival as we do. Animals exist alongside predators and prey, must negotiate complex economies ensuring their survival and the survival of their young, and have developed, highly evolved strategies to camouflage themselves by blending in with their environments, just like we do."

The following examples are excerpts from Dr. Faust's groundbreaking study titled "Things Pseudo-Native Authors Have Claimed to Be but Actually Are Not."

The Stick Insect

Some ways that pseudo-Indigenous authors have sought to capitalize on their careers is to disguise themselves as things that they are not. The biggest culprit is the stick insect—also referred to as walking sticks and stick bugs. Fraudulent Indigenous authors have acquired esteemed literary awards by camouflaging themselves as stick insects and mimicking branches and leaves. When necessary, they're masters in the art of invisibility while at the same time adapting to their environments in ingenious ways. Stick insects are known to adapt splendidly in unfamiliar terrains such as Indigenous literary conferences. Here they perform particularly well in panel and audience environments by remaining absolutely stationary, which enhances their disguise. One should exercise extreme caution when introduced to a stick insect due to its voracious appetites. Stick insects are known to bite the heads off of cohort of other species in competition for necessary resources such as literary prizes and fellowships and, when provoked, will also devour a rival's head whole.

The Chameleon

Included among the usual suspects is the chameleon. The chameleon's favorite habitat is the artist's colony or writer's residency. Here they've been known to thrive as their unique abilities of deception adapt beautifully to a variety of environments such as desert, mountain, or seascape. Their everyday skin color, a light khaki, keeps them hidden from enemies who would otherwise identify them and call them out, but they will change to whatever shade is necessary given the situation. They are extremely crafty when socializing at cocktail mixers, utilizing their ability to change color as surroundings shift. The chameleon/Native fraud can blend into the brightly colored tablecloths or barstools, making it easier for them to prey upon unwitting directors of reputable publishing houses or editors of endowed literary journals. They can manipulate with ease and will elicit pity from potential benefactors by relaying woeful tales of disenfranchisement and oppression.

Look for Dr. Faust's other books, *I'm Not an Actual Native Author but I Play One on* TV and *Checking the* It's Complicated Box *for Culture and/or Ethnicity.*

You Might Be a Pretendian

It seems like everyone and their great-grandmother wants to be Indian. This is nothing new. There's a name for folks who give off these mixed (smoke) signals: pretendians. From Iron Eyes Cody, Shania Twain, Justin Bieber, and Ward Churchill to Elizabeth Warren and Andrea Smith. Those are just a few. And let's not forget the over eighteen million questionable, self-proclaimed Cherokee tribes. Move over, Rachel Dolezal, pretendian culture is a national pastime with a long, celebrated history right up there with baseball, hot dogs, and apple pie. *It isn't just for breakfast anymore!*

Chances are if you're a pretendian, you are not aware that you're a pretendian. That's just part of the pretendian pathology. Remember Rachel from the sci-fi movie *Blade Runner*? Rachel didn't know she was a replicant; she believed that she was human. She was programmed to think she was human. The only thing convincing her otherwise was the irresistible Harrison Ford making her an offer she couldn't refuse.

Currently, there is no pretendian equivalent to *Blade Runner*'s "Voight-Kampff test"—the test used to identify replicant from human. And there is no official Native version of the old TV game show *To Tell the Truth*, called *Will the Real Native Please Stand Up*, though there totally should be, IMHO. So, until that time comes, I've created a checklist that should help to identify anyone who might be ethnically confused.

Are you a pretend Indian?

☐ You might be a pretendian if you write "high cheekbones" as proof of tribal citizenship when applying for a job.

☐ You might be a pretendian if Stands-with-a-Fist is your personal role model.

☐ You might be a pretendian if both of your parents emigrated from Germany.

☐ You might be a pretendian if you're in need of a dream catcher intervention.

☐ You might be a pretendian if you belong to a tribe that collects dues or is a registered nonprofit organization.

☐ You might be a pretendian if your grandmother never even met your supposed Indian ancestor.

☐ You might be a pretendian if you carry war paint in your purse.

☐ You might be a pretendian if you think blood quantum is measured in electron volts.

☐ You might be a pretendian if you have a wolf as a pet.

☐ You might be a pretendian if you wear your regalia to the gym to work out in.

☐ You might be a pretendian if you buy black hair dye by the case.

☐ You might be a pretendian if you feel entitled and expect Native people to sublet their intellectual property to you without a deposit.

☐ You might be a pretendian if you really, *really* love horses but haven't actually ridden one.

☐ You might be a pretendian if Disney's Pocahontas is your role model.

☐ You might be a pretendian if you've legally changed your name from Weissvogel to White Eagle Soaring.

☐ You might be a pretendian if you burn to a crisp in ten minutes of strong moonlight.

☐ You might be a pretendian if your star quilt was bought at Target or has Chewbacca on it.

☐ You might be a pretendian if you think immersing yourself in a rich, cultural experience means bathing in a bathtub full of yogurt.

☐ You might be a pretendian if you think "Idle No More" is a twelve-step anger support group.

☐ You might be a pretendian if you think you are better at being Native than any other Native person in history.

☐ You might be a pretendian if you cried during the movie *Avatar*.

☐ You might be a pretendian if you've had a tanning bed membership since 1992 and buy self-tanning lotion by the case.

☐ You might be a pretendian if you find your car at the mall's parking lot by following your trail of turquoise and abalone.

☐ You might be a pretendian if you say "aho" when getting your suv detailed and "in that good way" during meetings with your financial consultant.

☐ You might be a pretendian if you think sleeping with a Native person makes you Native by proximity.

* Stay tuned for "You Might Be a Super Indian if . . ."

VIII

I Watched
Woman Walks Ahead
and Frankly
Was Offended
by the Cookie-Cutter,
Stereotypical
Portrayal of the
Menacing White
Soldier

Reel Indians Don't Eat Quiche

The Fight for Authentic Roles in Hollywood

Hollywood needs to stop stereotyping Native Americans. Every time I see a new movie come out that features Native Americans, we're either wealthy hedge fund managers with a penchant for Italian automobiles or we're depicted as sexy surgeons who moonlight for Doctors Without Borders and adopt handicapped children from war-torn countries. Just stop it already! We're so much more than that!

Only rarely are we given a semblance of humanity. Take the film *The Revenant*, for instance. In the opening scenes, when a band of marauding Native Americans on horseback attacks a camp of innocent fur trappers, I was like, *finally*, filmmakers are making an effort to get this right! Some of the Native characters even wore loincloths. Whoa, that's some incisive storytelling right there. I thought, wow, the cultural consultants are spot on! Unfortunately, that isn't the norm, and it's time Hollywood started getting it right

Believe it or not, Native Americans are highly capable actors and have studied at reputable institutions with the best of them. Me, for instance, I studied at Juilliard and have an MFA in Theater Arts and Medieval Folk Dancing. I am more than willing to step outside of the same old, unimaginative typecasting of Native Americans as World War II SS officers and Nazi guards. It's as if Hollywood producers simply are not willing to see us beyond the clichés. How much longer do Native Americans have to get stuck playing roles like an eighteenth-century English shipping magnate or a Dutch textile industrialist before change can happen? If I see another sensitive and compelling biopic of Princess Diana or another Movie-of-the-Week portrayal of Marilyn Monroe played by [*insert famous Indigenous actor*], I'm going to totally lose my shit. It's just the same old colonialist narrative, the same old malarkey.

Some of the finest actors I know are Native American and can deliver an impressive range of characters, such as hostile savage Number 1 through 65 or housekeeper for wretched pill-popping matriarch. The shirtless, wolf pack portrayals in *Twilight* were some of the finest cinema of the last fifty years, beyond anything I've ever seen, even Wind in His Hair's breakout performance in *Dances with Wolves*.

Don't get me wrong: when I was just starting out, a naive, looks-good-without-a-shirt, ethnically ambiguous male actor, and I got my big break being cast as Gomer Pyle in the 2008 reboot of *Mayberry R.F.D.*, I was grateful for the work. And even though I was working with the whitest cast in the history of the world since *The Brady Bunch*, it was a solid credit. That's just the business; that's just how things are, I told myself. As the years have gone by, however, it's getting more difficult to settle. Take my role as Rory's love interest in *Gilmore Girls*. Naturally, the character of Rory Gilmore is going to date the richest playboy of the Atlantic Seaboard—it's a necessary arc of her character development—but the fact that *only* a Native American was considered for the role limits its scope and, frankly, makes it offensive. I was glad to get the role, but it was demoralizing too, what with the whole shopping with Rory at Bergdorf's and Tiffany's and those skiing trips in the Swiss Alps. Can you say *Hello! Pigeonhole much?!*

Thank god for the big blockbuster film companies! If it wasn't for the progressive-minded pioneers in giant movie conglomerates, our lives on the big screen would never be told, and Native Americans would forever be relegated to the same, stale codswallop we've been relegated to since the genesis of cinema. Native American actors deserve better, and so do the legions of moviegoers. I look amazing without a shirt. My war whoop is spot-on. I'm a champion equestrian and trained on the finest polo fields. Give me a chance.

Are You There, Christmas?
It's Me, Carol!

You might be surprised to learn that *Gremlins* is listed as a holiday movie. And in case you're like me and didn't already know, *Die Hard* and *Lethal Weapon* are also considered to be holiday treats, right up there with *It's a Wonderful Life* and *Miracle on 34rd Street*.

While those holiday gems might trigger ALL *of the feels*, they don't come anywhere near to warming the heart's cockles more than the Yuletide classic *Female Trouble*, starring the late great Divine, a family favorite also listed as a holiday go-to.

I don't know about you, but I'm still waiting for the NDN versions of the holiday classic movies. There are many, many adaptations of *A Christmas Carol*, all with extra special twists. SNL did a version with the hilarious Alec Baldwin lampooning Trump. I hoped that Donald "Scrooge" would be visited by the ghost of president past, Richard Nixon, who'd dispense some useful and sage advice, but he was visited by Putin instead.

I asked my boyfriend, "Who is the ghost of president future in the Donald 'Scrooge' story?" And faster than an elf can say ugly Christmas sweater in Lakota, he said "What future? Is there one?" Touché.

Along the same lines I'd like to see an NDN version of *A Christmas Carol* called *A Tradish-ish Tale*. A curmudgeonly tribal chairman, Caesar Beaucoup, played by Graham Greene, is visited by three ghosts, who make him realize the error of his ways and help him walk the red road to redemption and healing. The Bob Cratchit character could be played by Gary Farmer.

There's *How the Grinch Stole Christmas*, except Natives have been living out that timeless ode since Columbus first set foot on these shores. A more apt title might be *How the Whites Stole . . . Well, Everything*.

There's *Randolph the Red-Nosed Red*****, cousin to Chief Wahoo. But who can work up any sympathy for that chump?

How about *The Little Drummer Boy*? I've been singing a twisted version of this in my head forever! *Drum they told me, pa rum pum pum pum / But you have no blood quantum, you're a pretend-i-um-um* . . . it goes something like that. A bit contentious for the holidays, unless someone makes it a 49er.

I imagine a Nativity story taking place at Standing Rock called *A No DAPL Nativity*. Mary and Joseph Blackhorse, turned away at the Prairie Knight's Lodge, wander the plains almost out of gas and about to give birth. They follow a miraculous guided drone to Sacred Stone Camp, where good shepherds take them in.

I'd love to see a rez-style Christmas basketball tale called *Jingle Balls*. A ragtag team of rez misfits are about to go down in history as the worst ballers of all time. That is, until a mysterious coach in a Santa hat shows them the way to the state championships.

What about *Are You There, Christmas? It's Me, Carol!* A coming-of age mash-up of *Love Actually* and *Elf* but with robots. There's a scandal at the local shopping mall over the Black Santa. Ridiculous! Everyone knows Santa is a superalloy and vanadium steel AI with exterior epoxy resin.

And it wouldn't be Yuletide without the assorted Lifetime Christmas movies starring Meredith Baxter Birney or Tori Spelling. Movies with the word *danger* in them. Movies about mistaken identities and stepping barefoot on Legos in the middle of the night. Harrowing tales of intrigue and redemption. Movies about cards and candles and mistletoe and lovable ladies who overcome heartaches and hard times—movies with plucky gals like Dolly Parton, the ultimate Christmas angel, the quintessential fairy godmom of the rez.

Post-Election U.S. Open in Racist Tirades Competition

Announcer: We're coming at you live today from JCPenney Customer Service Desk here in Louisville, Kentucky, home to the Kentucky Derby, for the Post-Election U.S. Open in Racist Tirades Competition. Let me introduce the judges: first we have Tommy DeVito. Hello there Tommy, how are you doing?

Tommy DeVito: Why? Do I amuse you? Am I a clown? What exactly are you implying? Am I here for your amusement?

Announcer: Hahahaha, you're a live wire there, Tommy! And next we have Ann Coulter. Welcome to JCPenney's Customer Service, Ms. Coulter.

Ann Coulter: It's Ann, call me Ann. Only my mother calls me Ms. Coulter. Are there hors d'oeuvres? I was told there'd be hors d'oeuvres—I'm starving! I'm so hungry I could eat a live baby. Where are we again? JCPenney. People actually shop here for clothes!? What a shithole, what a dump.

Announcer: I'd like to introduce our final judge, Dolores Abernathy, who traveled here all the way from Westworld. Hello Dolores, thank you for being here today.

Dolores Abernathy [*smiles with her lovely eyes*]: Oh, hello. Some folks choose to only see the seedy underbelly of life. I choose to see the splendid panoramic sunsets.

Announcer: On deck for the racist rant competition today is Gladys Kasper, a Kentucky resident who made the news recently for directing a racist tirade at a pair of shoppers who were checking out in line ahead of her. Those shoppers happened to be Latina. Tommy, how would you rate her first maneuver? [*Shows clip of Gladys Kasper: "I think everybody here feels the same damn way I do!" Attempts to rally other shoppers in line, acknowledges someone's support, yells out "Thank you!" Stands defiantly, as if expecting applause.*]

Tommy DeVito: Weak. No guts at all. I would have burned it all down and collected the insurance money. One-half a point.

Ann Coulter: In my new book *Adios America: The Left's Plan to Turn Our Country into a Third World Shithole*, I very clearly state that America needs to secure the border! And it starts with J C P enney! There need to be blockades set up at *all* area resident shopping malls, like yesterday! I rate Gladys's first move a solid 10! Can I go higher than a 10? That grandma is tip-top in my book! Although she could use some styling advice—would it kill her to wear heels?

Dolores Abernathy: These violent delights have violent ends.

Announcer: And how many points do you wish to assign, Dolores?

Dolores Abernathy: We all love the newcomers. Every new person I meet reminds me how lucky I am to be alive . . . and how beautiful this world can be [*slaps fly*].

Tommy DeVito: That broad's a few fries short of a Happy Meal. I think she'd fold under questioning.

Announcer: Moving right along, here's a classic move by Gladys Kasper that we like to call "Stepping Back to the Jim Crow Era." [*Runs clip of Gladys addressing customer: "Go back to wherever the f**k you come from, lady." Clerk asks Gladys to watch her language." She responds: "Hey! Tell them to go back to where they belong!"*]

Tommy DeVito: You can trace immediate members of my family back to the old country. I'm proud of my immigrant roots. But those Latinx chicks—they're actually from here! Tell Gladys to go home; she's drunk! Zero. Zero points! The Mayans were among the first to invent zero, just saying.

Ann Coulter: As I wrote in my book *Adios America: The Left's Plan to Turn Our Country into a Third World Shithole*, America should be choosing immigrants like the New England Patriots choose players. They don't have a lottery system for draft picks. Solid 10! Give Gladys a medal! Extra point for use of colorful expletive! I wish I could say nothing but the *f*-word, but then no one would invite me to be on CNN and FOX News anymore.

Dolores Abernathy: Dear, dear, how queer everything is today. And yesterday things went on just as usual. I wonder if I've been changed in the night.

Announcer: Dolores? Would you like to offer a score?

Dolores Abernathy: Was I the same when I got up this morning? I almost think I can remember feeling a little different. But if I'm not the same, the next question is . . . who in the world am I?

Ann Coulter: I'll vote for Robot Girl—can I have her vote? 10. All of my little piggies, 10, 10, 10!

Announcer: Next, Gladys Kasper ups the ante. [*Runs clip: "Just because you come from another country doesn't make you special—get in the back of line like everybody else! The taxpayers probably pay for all that stuff!"*] Tommy, how do you rate this play?

Tommy DeVito: Gladys needs to stop busting everybody's balls before someone hits her with a fricken shinebox.

She's bought her fricken button. Again, nuttin', I got nuttin'. Zero.

Ann Coulter: In my book . . .

Tommy DeVito: Again with the book plug! Lady, no one's interested in your damn book. Just say your score so we can all get out of here, get our checks, and call it a day, all right already!

Ann Coulter: Wait? You were told we're getting a check? I wasn't told I was getting a check. I was told I could promote my book. Hey . . .

Announcer: . . . And now it's time for a break from our sponsor! We'll be right back . . . [*Crash heard coming from offstage, incoherent yelling, Ann Coulter throws chair at Tommy DeVito's head.*]

Dolores Abernathy: I think there may be something wrong with this world. Something hiding underneath. Either that or . . . or there's something wrong with me. I may be losing my mind . . . [*Screen goes black.*]

West Wing World

Dear West Wing World Guest,

Hello and welcome to West Wing World, your immersive resort and holiday experience. I'm Kellyanne, your personal concierge. We hope you enjoyed our West Wing World transit accommodations. If you were stalked or nearly taken prisoner by staffer holdouts from the Obama administration, please accept our apologies. We are still in the process of evacuating hosts and personnel who have been . . . shall we say, a teensy bit confused about the concept of "changing of the guard." Obama left gracefully, but former VP Biden has holed up in a cupboard on the third floor like Anne Frank and refuses to leave. Our security teams have assured us that you're in no danger. In fact, some of our guests are quite exhilarated by all the excitement and have even requested that former VP Biden take them as hostages. Here at West Wing World we aim to please. That's our motto, right up there with "alternative facts."

If you are viewing this orientation video, congratulations! You made it! I am here to ensure that your stay will be as enjoyable as possible. Should you need any assistance, please contact me anytime, day or night. (Like seriously, day or night—I literally don't sleep or have any personal agency whatsoever; usually, I try and keep that on the DL because some guests find it rather creepy, but

I can tell right away that you're different from all the rest, and I really mean that, wink.)

Soon you will be escorted to West Wing World's Wardrobe and Personas Suite. The park is all-inclusive, and clothing from Ivanka's fashion and accessories line, which is official dress code for West Wing World staff, awaits you, along with everything you need to enjoy your stay. Speaking of fascists . . . excuse me, I mean fashion, we are excited to launch a line of Hawaiian shirts, just $2,999.00 each, and elastic waist cargo shorts, only $4,999.00, under President Steve Bannon's brand. The cargo shorts are perfect for stashing executive orders and those discreet flasks of Stolichnaya. Buy them today while supplies last!

We apologize for the rabid mob of professional protesters in pussy headgear outside the gates. We understand how distressing lady people can be, especially lady people without the ability to properly accessorize or mix and match appropriate separates from Ivanka Trump's fashion line. You'll receive no such guff from our lady hosts here at West Wing World—we know our place, and we salute the gumption of Oklahoma legislators and encourage other districts to follow suit because we understand that our bodies belong to the state, and we put the *host* in *hostess*, especially pregnant lady bodies. Your special man seed is our parasite and our pleasure! Blessed be the fruit!

We hope you've had the opportunity to review the Storyline Itineraries located in your orientation handbooks. Please make your selections and choose your safe words.

DAY 1: The transit pod will deposit you at the White House West Wing, a bustling administrative community full of character and charm. West Wing World is a step back into a time when *America was great,* back to those halcyon days when women couldn't buy property and minorities couldn't vote or be within fifty yards of a white person. If you're looking for a glimpse of Russian interference, explore the communications room or check out President Bannon's office.

DAY 2: Time to expand your horizons by climbing aboard a horse and buggy for a visit to the State Department, a close-knit community you're not sure to forget. Just pay mind that you have boarded the right buggy—they are clearly marked "Whites Only" and "Others/Minorities."

DAY 3: If you're up for some adventure, head over to the East Wing. You will pass through the west and east colonnades, the perfect place for hiking, animal watching, and mining for gold. Be on the lookout for ghosts and haunts—the East Wing's Jackie O. Garden is built on an ancient Indian graveyard!

DAY 4: *Time to lean in* where you'll discover one of the park's most timeless perks: guilt-free decadence. Check out the Situation Room, where you can verbally abuse world leaders, like Mexican president Peña Nieto, without censure. Or have fun accusing Australian prime minister Turnbull of dumping terrorist onto the United States and then hang up on him. Attacking other countries is unpresidented.

DAY 5: In the midst of all the action, park guests often overlook undiscovered areas, such as the Tweets Hall of Fame Toilet. Here you'll view a photo gallery of some of the president's most memorable Tweets while he was taking his midmorning constitutionals. Who could forget such sage wisdom—like when the president addressed

U.S. judge James Robart's halting of the restricted travel ban, in all caps: "SEE YOU IN COURT, THE SECURITY OF OUR NATION IS AT STAKE!" Or who could forget: "The FAKE NEWS media (failing @nytimes, @NBCNews, @ABC, @CBS, @CNN) is not my enemy, it is the enemy of the American People!" Tweet your own unforgettable fake news!

DAY 6: After nearly a week in the park, you might be ready to explore. The more experienced park visitor might enjoy Mar-a-Lago, or what the president refers to as the "Southern White House," in Palm Beach, Florida. Here the president spends long weekend vacations on the tax-payers' dime. Or if you have a hankering for Manhattan, venture over to Melania Trump's sanctuary in the Trump Tower—another ringing example of taxpayer fleecing, at the cost of only a half-million dollars per day to maintain.

DAY 7: A whole week in, and you've just started to uncover all that West Wing World has to offer. Have you visited Congress yet? Plenty of mudslinging and stone-walling sure to delight! We hope you enjoyed the special luncheon with Frederick Douglass in observance of African American History Month. Mr. Douglass is doing a terrific job! Visit us again next season, when we'll be hosting a banquet in honor of Native American Heritage Month with special guests Elizabeth "Pocahontas" Warren and Andrew Jackson.

Our hosts are here to fulfill your every desire and look forward to serving you. Have a wonderful time. The wild, untamed landscape awaits.

IX

The Native
Americans
Used EVERY Part
of the Sacred
Turkey

Hey America,
I'm Taking Back Thanksgiving

November 2016

Hey America,

Well, it's been fun. We've had a good run. But we're done now. No hard feelings—it's just not working out. It's not you; it's me, okay? Well, actually it is you, but whatevs. If it's cool with you, I'd like to drop by your place when you're at work tomorrow so I can get my stuff. Where's that bootleg of Cold Play? It has sentimental value, so I hope you can find it. I also want my Gorge 2014 T-shirt back. I know I said we'd share it, but Dave Matthews played that year, and after you drove us into a telephone pole at Marblemount last summer, I feel I've more than earned my rights to it—think of it as a kind of Dave Matthews Doctrine of Discovery claim.

Anyway, I'm breaking up with you. I know I said I was in it for the long haul, and I know we've been through a lot together, blah blah blah, but you've really crossed a line this time and, like, disrespected a ton of my most deeply felt principles. You broke me, America. You broke us. Like HULK SMASHED our relationship to indecipherable shards. Like you pulled a Humpty Dumpty, and nobody's horses and king's men are putting us back together. Consider us toothpaste squeezed out of the tube. Done. Kaput. Take the cannoli.

I think you know why. But I'll explain in the interest of transparency. Recently, when President Obama proclaimed the month of November to be National Native American Heritage Month and then the very next day in an interview about the Dakota Access Pipeline and paramilitary police waging war against citizens at Standing Rock—stating that he was going to "just let it play out for several more weeks"—well, that hurt. Maybe it didn't hurt as much as the mace and pepper spray or the people who got shot with rubber bullets, but still, *dude*, so not cool.

Lately, too, there's just been injustice piled on top of injustice piled on top of injustice. It's like a Russian doll of injustice. Or a Dagwood sandwich of injustice. A totem pole of injustice. Mass shootings, cop killers getting off, ominous clown sightings, folk singers awarded Noble Prizes in literature, baseball fans cheering the Cleveland Indians while actual Indians are being terrorized in North Dakota, and WTAF, America? Donald Trump winning the presidential election?! Really? Really? You're twisted, America. You've gone cuckoo banana pants.

So, anyway, here's the deal. In addition to my Gorge T-shirt and my Cold Play bootleg, I'm taking back Thanksgiving. It was mine to begin with; you were just appropriating it to satisfy your need for some happy-go-lucky fairy tale in the midst of crimes against humanity. Yep, the real Thanksgiving was FUBAR, a real shit-show, and sorry, but you're totes culpable. You might as well start dealing with it. No turkey for you. I'm taking it back. Admit it, you never liked it all that much anyway, unless it was deep fat fried in the back yard, and that's an obscene thing to do to poultry.

No more cranberries, no more stuffing. And that roasted brussels sprout dish your grandma makes with the pumpkin seeds sprinkles, I'm taking that too. I'm taking back the sweet potato dish with the mini-marshmallows on top, and I'm taking back the mashed potatoes. I'm taking back the pumpkin pie and the mincemeat and the whipped cream. You can keep the green bean casserole, though. If I wanted to stroke out, I'd do better hooking myself up to a sodium and preservatives IV drip. I hope you choke on it. No offense to your mom.

In case you're worried, you'll be comforted to know that I won't be taking your precious NFL Thursday games. The Redskins are set to face the Cowboys at Jerry World this year, and I'm sure you're completely over the moon about that abomination. You can even dress up in your redface and feather warbonnet and piss yourself up and down till Sunday for all I care. It's your stupid day. You can do whatever you want. But I'm taking back Thanksgiving.

Don't worry about my share of the rent. I think I've been paying more, like way, way more than my fair share the last five hundred–plus years. But I'm doing you a solid and paying the cable and Netflix because I'm the one who ordered it, and I'm the one who can't get enough of *Stranger Things* and *The Walking Dead*. Yeah, sure, America, you did some things right—your television programming is tip-top, especially *Lost*, and *Black Mirror*, but whatevs. You're welcome.

Don't bother trying to get back with me or leaving me passive-aggressive messages on all my friend's Facebook pages. I've already blocked you. Don't Tweet me, don't message me, don't call. We're done. I hope you figure yourself out and someday get your life and your country together. Good luck.

Yours Not-So-Truly Anymore,
Tiffany

P.S. I flirted with Canada for a while behind your back, but they're not working out either, so don't even think of looking for me there. I've moved on.

Clown Costumes Banned, Racist Native American Halloween Costumes Still Okay

Prompted by a creepy clown threat posted on a Colorado student's Facebook account, along with the onslaught of creepy clown sightings and situations occurring all across the country in two dozen states, several Colorado public schools have imposed a ban on clown costumes and apparel from school property. No big red squeaky noses, no giant daisy flowers that spurt water, no oversized clown shoes. It's a very sad day at the circus.

Denver Public Schools issued the following statement: "In an effort to minimize the concern for students, families, and educators, the district is banning all clown masks and clown makeup from our schools, school grounds, and athletic facilities during this Halloween season."

While it's understandable that clown costumes would be banned from public spaces—they are, after all, terrifying to many people who suffer from coulrophobia, clown phobia—but what's more difficult to understand is that racist Native American–inspired costumes are perfectly acceptable. Native social justice activists have been speaking out against Native American–themed costumes for many years now, yet companies still churn them out, and stores still order and sell them. When I contacted the costume supply store in my small town and complained, the owner said that they couldn't afford to stop selling them, that their Pocahottie, Indian Brave, and Big Chief costumes were their top sellers for Halloween.

Colorado school Brighton 27J reportedly decided to ban clown costumes, believing that it is the best way to avoid perpetuating clown fear or paranoia. Another school, Adams 12, has also issued a prohibition encouraging parents to discuss the power of social media because that was where the clown problem all started.

Should McDonald's mascot clown, Ronald McDonald, be outlawed? Should authorities place an embargo on Jack in the Box? These are good questions, but an even better question is: WTF, universe? Why are there menacing clown reports in two dozen states since April? And why are scary clowns more threatening than say, well, I don't know, *racism*?

It's a matter of perspective I suppose, right?

This development somewhat reminds me of when Cecil the Lion was killed and the international media attention and outrage that resulted. Feminist author Roxane Gay responded with her now famous Tweet for how to draw attention to police violence in America—violence that has overwhelmingly impacted black men, women, and children. She Tweeted, "I'm personally going to start wearing a lion costume when I leave my house so if I get shot, people will care."

While no one would dream of tailoring a Pocahottie, Chief, or Indian Brave costume to sinister ends—I mean, what would that even look like? And aside from the fact that the existence of those costumes are already heinous and disturbing enough to Native people, would dressing up in Native American–inspired costumes and lurking around the edges of housing developments and neighborhood parks be enough to cause a public crisis? Would taking back the image of a *bloodthirsty savage* strike fear and panic in the hearts of ordinary citizens? Would roving Pocahottie hordes be enough to banish such costumes for Halloween or even forever?

"In the news today sinister-looking Pocahotties were spotted lurking outside a wooded area near an apartment complex . . ."

"Keep your children and pets indoors tonight, an ominous-looking Tonto with a giant bird on his head was seen near Forest Glen public park this evening . . ."

"A man dressed in a noble warrior deluxe Native American costume was reported last evening crouching among trees . . ."

Last month Disney's offensive Moana skin suit with tattoos costumes were pulled from the shelves. That represents a glimmer of progress.

Addendum: In September 2018 the online retail company Yandy immediately pulled its sexy handmaid's costume from its website after widespread backlash but, after repeated protest and petitions from Native American critics, refused to stop selling its sexy Native and Pocahottie costumes. Native activist groups and allies have been campaigning against the selling of these costumes for several years, as costumes contribute to the oppression and dehumanization of Indigenous people, similar to Indian sports mascots such as the NFL's Washington Redskins and school sports teams.

Thanksgiving Shopping at Costco

I Just Can't Even

Once or twice a month I treat my nana to lunch at Costco for the rounds of free samples. I tell her we're at Old Country Buffet, and she's none the wiser. She's a big fan of the crescent rolls and pot stickers. Sometimes we hit the food court on the way out for 99-cent hot dogs and the all-you-can-eat onions and relish "salad" bar. It's about all the excitement her sweet little heart can take, so I try and ration it out. But, hey, it's Costco! It's well worth the risk of a potential cardiac event.

Costco is the gettin' place for holiday feast fixins. It gets pretty crazy with shoppers this time of year. But I don't go for any of that since I don't celebrate Thanksgiving. Instead, I act out a version of *How the Grinch Stole Thanksgiving*. Maybe you have one of me in your circle of friends or colleagues? Sound familiar? I'm one of those sanctimonious guests at the table offering anecdotes about the *real* Thanksgiving. I admit, I'm a real wet blanket, especially after my lecture on misappropriation on Halloween, my speeches on Columbus Day, and my throwdown about Veterans Day for good measure.

The last few years I've frequented Costco for the gourmet foods in bulk. It's where I buy my figs. And since my truffle allergies make it nearly impossible to enjoy a decent meal, I buy a Costco brand of truffle oil that my delicate system can handle. I also shop there to refresh my supply of hardback copies of Jodi Picoult and Nicholas Sparks books—artisanal crafted romance novels, white tears included, no extra charge. Good value! Speaking of white tears, this last trip I stocked up on economy-sized packs of safety pins, ten thousand count—those should get me to the next election, provided Mr. Pumpkin Head doesn't nuke us first. A tragic waste of safety pins, if you ask me, so I hope that orange windigo can keep his shit together. Speaking of romance novels and the election, the other day it occurred to me how our current state of affairs is like a chapter from *Flowers in the Attic*: the American people are the tragic children locked up in the attic, and the goblin in chief is our mom's new boyfriend she's going to whack us for. I just hope everyone is saved in time before we're forced to put out mousetraps or take turns feeding on Brother Bannon's alcohol-infused blood.

You know, I swear I saw Melania Trump shopping at Costco last week. I can't imagine what she was doing in Clarkston, Washington, but you never know. She was clacking around the warehouse in her stiletto heels, shoving other shoppers out of the way, pushing her customized, dipped-in-gold shopping cart filled with Goodrich tires and bulk economy-sized packages of kielbasa sausages and mini-chandeliers. She indulged in the sample buffet, threw her head back, unhinged her jaw like a reptile, and swallowed whole trays. It was quite impressive. People applauded. If this First Lady thing doesn't work out, she could apply at a carnival sideshow.

Any day now I expect a new reality show to air on the Lifetime Channel called *The Billionaire and the Showgirl in the White House*. It will star Melania and Donald and their menagerie of sprog, bootlickers, and erstwhile ne'er-do-wells. Episode 1: "Ted Nugent and Duck Dynasty for a Roadkill Brunch." Episode 2: "State Dinners with Tila Tequila and Dennis Rodman." Episode 3: "A Very Special Thanksgiving with Scott Baio and the All-White Cast of *Hamilton*." Their reality show will be reminiscent of the *Beverly Hillbillies*. Tiffany Trump should play Elly May; she can install an official White House chicken coop and sell golden eggs by the dozen to visiting emissaries. When the hens fail to lay gold, Tiffany will spectacularly melt down like Veruca Salt just before the Oompa Loompas haul her away.

Did you see Melania's erotic photos? A friend said that the photos are actually progressive. I would agree. But a lot of people don't remember that centerfold spread featuring Barbara Bush or those tasteful nudes of Lady Bird Johnson in *Juggs*. Melania, our future First Naked Lady. Right. It's said that Americans have a short memory, and I believe it. Except, of course, when it comes to Hillary's emails.

It makes a peculiar kind of sense that Thanksgiving, Costco, and Trump have all come together at this point in time. When I think of Costco, I think of excess, bigly, yuge! And when I think of Thanksgiving, I think of people like Trump—Trump is the personification of imperialism, a fat taker; he puts the *colon* in *colonialism* and worse.

Politically Correct Alternatives to Culturally Insensitive Halloween Costumes

Have you been thinking about dressing up as Pocahontas, your favorite Disney princess, this Halloween but feel like it wouldn't be socially acceptable? Well, I feel you; that's rough. You could wear a sexy Sacagawea costume and go as a racist like your RA so cleverly suggested, but what does she know, anyway? She's majoring in social justice studies. Is there even a department for that? People probably wouldn't get it, anyway. Subtlety is a lost art, and postmodern doesn't translate well when you're holding an ace in an epic round of pass the doody.

Hey, if you ask me, people are way too sensitive. I mean, just because you love putting on a feather headdress made in China and war whooping and shouting, "Make it rain, make it rain!" at Octoberfest—or whatever music festivals you attend with Horsey-face, the cousin your mom makes you do stuff with because your aunt paid for that Alaskan cruise—doesn't make you racist. There's cultural insensitivity, and then there's being racist. There's a big difference, am I right?

Don't be too butt hurt about that faux buckskin loincloth collecting dust in the back of your closet. And I know you were stoked about wearing that Disney tattooed skin suit and flouncing around at the gravel pit kegger like Jame Gumb to Goodbye Horses, but hear me out. I have some creative solutions. There's a bunch of politically correct alternatives to choose from; I mean, you don't want to be labeled supremo douchebag of the year, do you? Yeah, I know, political correctness blows. Yep, I saw that Bill Maher segment too. Bear with me, okay? Here are just a few, totally random suggestions. No presh.

Scary clown. Alternative: Assistant manager at Just a Buck! Dollar Store, where EVERYTHING'S JUST A BUCK! OR I'LL EAT MY HAT! Or as your dad calls it, the Dollar Store, island of misfit toiletries.

Cholo/a. Alternative: Euphemia, the vanpool lady at your summer job last year who wore a crucifix bigger than her head and always smelled like Vicks and cherry-flavored Lip Smacker.

Muslim suicide bomber. Alternative: Marilyn Monroe from *The Seven Year Itch*, after her divorce from Joe DiMaggio but just before she started studying the Stanislavski method.

Day of the Dead sugar skull. Alternative: Goth version of Tiffany Trump.

Sexy geisha. Alternative: Caucasian fusion food truck owner with a topknot who owes over a hundred thou in defaulted student loans but will still buy artisanal truffle oil and imported bird's nests from intrepid caves in Southeast Asia.

Pocahottie. Alternative: Minneapolis police deputy who diligently works extra shifts to pay for Daphne's braces and keep that no-good joke of a husband in Pall Malls and Blue Nun.

Pimp daddy in blackface. Alternative: Rachel Dolezal. Or is that too edgy?

Hillbilly. Alternative: Lumbersexual with anachronistic mustache and overly gimmicky bow tie who eschews iPhones and won't shut up about it.

Harambe. Alternative: Ken Bone à la Stuart Smalley à la your eighth grade biology teacher, Mr. Phillips, whom you asked, "What is the difference between an organism and an orgasm?"

Caitlyn Jenner. Alternative: Wonder Woman. Too easy.

South Pacific hula dancer. Alternative: Eleven from *Stranger Things*.

Romani person mistakenly referred to as a "Gypsy." Alternative: Mrs. Roper from *Three's Company* but a conceptual version, like just Mrs. Roper's housedress and a completion certificate from DeVry University in personnel management.

Seriously, dude? What are you waiting for—any one of these would be rad. Good luck and Happy Halloween!

X

BREAKING NEWS—Your Neighbor Who Said, "Whoa, Dude, This Whole Trump Thing's, Like, So Fricken Surreal," Might Actually Be on to Something

Step Right Up, Folks

By the time of this reading, our country will have entered a new era. Hold your loved ones close. I'm talking about Inauguration Day, or as my anti-Trump comrades would call it, "The Day the Earth Stood Still." Or the opening ceremony for *The Hunger Games*. Or a lesser-known title, *Bury My Heart at Boo-Boo's Big, Fat, Circus Jubilee*. I kind of feel sorry for the guy whose job it was to pass out barf bags at the inauguration: "What size do you need? Small, medium, or infinity?"

Personally, I'm in a state of numb incredulity, when locked-in-a-fetal-position would be a more appropriate response. The incoming administration shares much in common with horror movies and dystopian disaster films, and like horror movies and dystopian disaster films, it would be a lot easier to suspend my incredulity if the imperiled shit their pants and it was part of the dialogue. But whatever your response or lack of response may be—pants shitting or fetal positioning—it'd be super if we could just fast-forward and montage the next four years into a series of brief clips in which nobody gets hurt.

Lately, there's been no shortage of despair. I count myself among those who are mourning—it's as if my spirit animal slayed and consumed my emotional support animal. Some folks say they're going to pull a Johnny Cash and wear only black for the next four years as a sign of distress. I say stick to bright colors—we need them. Others have ramped up their wardrobe selections for the inauguration. For those in disbelief and various stages of grief, here's some fashion tips: choose accessories that will flatter your hysteria and go well with your nonstop screaming. Are you a Spring? If you're shopping for shoes, go for ones that can transition from canvassing for human rights by day to post-inaugural nonstop sobbing by night. And if you're looking for that perfect inaugural dress, go for something that matches your eyes and the four horses of the Apocalypse. Avoid matchy-matchy and choose colors that pop, like a handful of Wellbutrin.

And as if there aren't enough examples to add to the carnival atmosphere as of late, the infamous 146-year-old Ringling Bros. and Barnum & Bailey Circus announced it's drawing its curtains and dismantling its big top. Never fear, however, there's a new circus in town—the Trump administration. Send in the clowns.

It's a well-known fact that when one loses their eyesight or hearing, the other senses will compensate to pick up the slack. This is 100 percent true! I've been noticing lately that as my body deteriorates, my sense of moral outrage increases. Yep. Send in the clowns. Uh, don't bother—they're here.

Trump Pardons Zombie Apocalypse

In August 2017 white nationalists protested in a Unite the Right rally in Charlottesville, Virginia. The protest left over thirty people injured and one woman dead. President Trump minimized the destructive rally by stating to the press that the white nationalists included "some very fine people." And placed blame on both the perps and the victims: "We condemn in the strongest possible terms this egregious display of hatred, bigotry, and violence on many sides. On many sides."

WASHINGTON DC—President Trump pardoned the Zombie Apocalypse on Tuesday, stating that the zombies who in 2015 had wreaked havoc in the streets by attacking and eating people's brains "were just doing their job."

The president's order has stirred an outcry from the Centers for Disease Control and Prevention, the National Institute of Public Health, the Department of Health, and law enforcement agencies. "This sets a very poor precedent for any future zombie attacks," said the director of public health, Carrie OnLugguge. "This is a horrible example of leadership. THIS IS NOT NORMAL."

President Trump Tweeted: "I want to set the record straight. I condemn marauding, violence, and flesh eating, on many sides. On many sides."

A spokesman for the Centers for Disease Control and Prevention responded: "Did I read that right? Did the president claim that 'both sides do it—'? He is clearly cuckoo for Cocoa Puffs.

This is not a 'zombies do this and the living do that' kind of situation. The walking dead eat brains and not with a bottle of nice Chianti and some fava beans but violently and immorally. The living were innocent victims. There's no sides to it."

According to sources, President Trump did not consult with the Justice Department. The pardon is President Trump's first, and he did not follow through with protocols set by the Obama administration before announcing his decision.

A spokesman for the Zombie Apocalypse stated in a Tweet: "Thank you @DTrump for cutting thru the bologna, this was a political witch hunt instigated by the Obama administration."

The Zombie Apocalypse continues to receive criticism from the Democratic Party and its liberal constituents. President Trump minimized their concerns by Tweeting: "Zombies are so hot now, I don't see what the problem is. I'll make a prediction: I think it's going to be just fine, okay?"

There's Something about Andrew Jackson

President Donald Trump laid his body down and drifted into a necromantic state at the tomb of Andrew Jackson last week in Nashville, Tennessee. Prior to the visit, which was planned to commemorate Jackson's 250th birthday, President Trump consulted a witch doctor and held a séance in the Oval Office with his closest cabinet members.

A White House spokesperson said: "The president is seeking a spiritual allegiance with the seventh U.S. Indian killer . . . uh, I mean president. He's been trying to conjure Andrew Jackson since even before he took office. I mean, he just *loves* the guy! It's a regular bromance, despite the fact Jackson is dead. I mean, all I can say about their relationship status is that it's complicated."

In his first week in office President Trump hung a portrait of Andrew Jackson in the Oval Office. Trump described his honorable master in a set of Tweets: "Some people might consider Jackson an unearthly beast, a black stain upon the universe, a reveler in anarchy and wickedness among the enclaves of darkness and shadows, but I think people should give him a chance! Jackson's a great guy!"

White House insiders report that Trump has papered his private quarters with posters and images of the homicidal tyrant and appears to be carrying out dark rituals in the evenings between watching Fox News and tapes of *The Apprentice*. Details of the rituals are sketchy, but there are reports that they involve certain farm animals and rolls of aluminum foil.

Other accounts from housekeeping staff say that the president is often heard repeating "Andrew Jackson" over and over. "The president seems to believe Andrew Jackson is Beetlejuice. You don't want to mess with that Beetlejuice dude—that's a bad, bad hombre, and he's kind of disgusting. I mean, have you seen his teeth?"

Andrew Jackson is the United States' seventh president and a figure who many people, including Choctaw citizen Aaron Butler, believe to be evil incarnate: "Andrew Jackson makes Jeffrey Dahmer look like an amateur. The United States and the president are essentially valorizing Jeffrey Dahmer. Imagine having the portrait of Jeffrey Dahmer on the twenty-dollar bill. What are you laughing at? I don't think that's funny—I think that's sick. Get out of my face!"

The last president known to conjure the spirit of Andrew Jackson was Ronald Reagan, when he visited Jackson's Tennessee Hermitage in 1982. Later that year Nancy Reagan fell into a well.

Trump Administration to Repeal Bison as First National Mammal

WASHINGTON DC—The Trump administration plans to overturn the National Bison Legacy Act, a legislative bill that passed the House and Senate last April that unanimously approved the bison as the first national mammal of the United States. President Obama signed the bill into law.

In a statement to the press Trump said: "Buffaloes are tremendous animals, just huge, they're great with baked potatoes, but we can do better as a nation. I have appointed Donald Jr. and Eric on the task force for repealing the buffaloes and choosing a better animal. They'll do a great job—they love animals."

Donald Jr. and Eric Trump stirred controversy in recent months when the press released photographs of the pair posing with exotic animals they shot and killed during pleasure-hunting expeditions in Africa.

"First things first," President-elect Trump said. "There's so much damage to undo. Obama's work on this country has been a disaster, just a disaster. We've got a big job ahead of us, just slash and burn, slash and burn. Make America great again, bigly."

The jury's still out as to whom Trump will appoint to head the Department of the Interior. Initial reports indicated the assignment might go to former governor of the State of Alaska Sarah Palin. Trump was interested in Governor Palin because of her prior experience with the Aerial Wolf Killing Program. "What a tremendous thing the Aerial Wolf Killing Program would be for the Lower 48 in controlling the buffaloes and wild horses," Trump stated.

The bison joined the bald eagle as a national symbol. Both animals represent our nation's regard for wildlife conservation. Groups tapped in selecting the buffalo as the official mammal were conservationists, ranchers, and the Intertribal Buffalo Council. It is the wishes of the Intertribal Buffalo Council to restore bison to Indian nations to observe and practice their spiritual and cultural beliefs and traditions.

President-elect Trump stated, "If it was just up to me, I'd choose the warthog as America's national mammal." When told that the warthog is a type of wild pig found living in open habitats in sub-Saharan Africa, Trump paused, then stated: "Well, the alligator then. They make great handbags. Ivanka sells them—they're yuge."

President Trump Scheduled for Whirl-wind Tour to Desecrate World's Treasures

On November 27, 2017, during National Native American Heritage Month, beneath a portrait of Andrew Jackson, President Trump insulted Native Americans during a ceremony to honor Navajo code talkers by wisecracking about his "Pocahontas" moniker for Senator Elizabeth Warren.

WASHINGTON DC —President Trump is scheduled over the next several months to tour the treasures and masterpieces of the world for the purpose of dumping a steaming pile of crap upon them.

A White House insider stated: "The president is really excited about dropping trou and taking dumps around the world. He is particularly looking forward to pinching a deuce at the Louvre next to the statue of Venus de Milo. I believe the president indicated 'he had a bigly for that broad with no arms.'"

The president will visit the Vatican at the first of the year to drop some kids off at the pool. And from there he plans to make a Yule log at Rome's Colosseum, curl some pipe at the Great Pyramid of Giza, download some brownware at the Great Wall of China, and launch a butt shuttle at the Taj Mahal, before squatting a rocket at Christ the Redeemer.

The president's worldwide pooparama is predicted to have low turnouts, much like his inauguration, despite what the president expects.

XI

The Trump
Administration's
Pop-Up,
Coloring,
Scratch 'n' Sniff,
Edible,
and Radioactive
Activity Book

You've Got Mail!

I. Did. Not. Dine. Alone. With. That. Female.
— vp Mike Pence

Vice President Mike Pence was in the hot seat last week. It was confirmed that Pence used a private email account through AOL to conduct public business while serving as Indiana's governor.

A Washington source said: "Hello! Pot calling kettle black. The GOP couldn't shut up for one second about Secretary Clinton's emails and private server, and then this doofus handles discretionary information on his AOL account? Who uses AOL? Was the Pony Express closed for repairs? Did he run out of pennies for sending a telegraph?"

In addition to Pence's AOL account, other reports have surfaced regarding vp Pence's Myspace page, "MikeyLikesIt"—a title taken from a popular 1970s LIFE cereal commercial about a finicky kid who hates everything—and Pence's LiveJournal blog, "Need for Speed, Maverick's Blog," in reference to the film *Top Gun*.

Pence's spokesman said: "Mike Pence is a politician with the soul of a poet, and deep down he's hardcore emotive. A lot of people don't know that Mike spends his free time writing fan fic and posting it on his LiveJournal blog. A lot of his stories involve erotic situations between characters from *X-Men*."

It was also reported that vp Pence enjoys using his Myspace page to share "killer tunes" with his staff and constituents. A Myspace friend said: "Yeah, he's into sweet guitar licks, and some of his favorite groups are Jawbreaker and Sunny Day Real Estate. I can take it or leave his posts, though. He, like, posts a shit ton of Winnie the Pooh and Ariel the Mermaid Princess memes. Those, like, aren't even ironic, you know? He just really likes them."

White House officials are considering stripping Pence of his security clearance, and souvenir retailers are now selling LOCK HIM UP T-shirts and tote bags on the National Mall.

Executive Order Requiring All Americans Take Up Cigarettes by End of 2017

WASHINGTON DC—President Trump signed an executive order requiring all U.S. citizens, even minors and children, to take up cigarettes or "use" tobacco products by the end of 2017. If citizens do not comply, they risk jail time or pay severe penalties up to $250,000.

Little is known of how this executive order will be monitored, but there is speculation that some kind of incentive program will be put in place. Secretary of Education Betsy DeVos has plans under way to take covert, on-the-sly smoking out of school bathrooms and into the open—just as soon as the Department of Education figures out this whole gender-specific restroom thing.

A White House spokesperson said: "Tobacco is good for the American economy. The tobacco industry creates jobs. It's un-American not to use tobacco. Those so-called reports that smoking is bad for your health are simply a matter of fake news."

Tobacco products are the leading cause of cancer and other health diseases, including heart disease, stroke, and emphysema. Cigarettes are known to contain several carcinogenic chemicals, including arsenic and formaldehyde. Also, the world is flat, and the Easter Bunny is real.

Responding to the dangers of cigarettes, the president reportedly said: "It's just another scare tactic, like so-called climate change. Fake news. If global warming was real, then how come it's snowing in that place with the green ground and big sky—you know that outside place with the wolf puppies and baby bears and stuff? Those are some bad, bad hombres."

The mandatory smoking order followed up the order to dismantle the Stream Protection Rule, a safeguard crafted to protect clean water and the health of communities threatened by coal mining. Republican lawmakers overturned the protection rule using the Congressional Review Act, a seldom used law that removes the public from the process by allowing rollbacks on recently finalized regulations.

The president mentioned to a White House staffer that he plans for Americans to stop eating fruits and vegetables in addition to Americans taking up smoking. "The deportation mandates of those who live and work in our country will assist bigger tariffs on Mexican imports and no farm workers working illegally to harvest crops. Who likes fruits and vegetables, anyway? Nobody, that's who. Vitamins and minerals are fake news."

The Wild West (Wing) and Wild Bill Hiccup

I read in the *New York Times* last month that President Trump, aka Wild Bill Hiccup, spent the afternoon of his second day in office poring over the White House's art collection and selecting a painting with which to grace the Oval Office. I imagine him asking himself, Which painting *defines* me? What will best represent my great and powerful brand? Who is the bigliest of them all, besides myself? He finally settled on a portrait of Andrew Jackson, notorious mass murderer, a historical figure whom Trump clearly admires.

How did Ronald McDonald, insane clown president in chief, come to this conclusion about Andrew Jackson, anyway? I imagine Trump sitting alone in the White House kitchen with his bachelor dinner of steak tartare with catsup, fava beans, and a nice Chianti and enjoying a documentary about Andrew Jackson on the History Channel. If the idea of the president watching anything other than Fox News is too implausible, then let's say that someone unloaded a pair of *Bloody Bloody Andrew Jackson* tickets on him instead. I don't imagine Trump would have liked the play—he might have been misled to assume it featured The Rockettes or the Mormon Tabernacle Choir.

According to the *New York Times*, many close to Trump have drawn parallels between him and Andrew Jackson, calling Trump a natural successor to Jackson, referring to both as "men of the people" and hallmarks of political populism. Yet who knows what the attraction is? It is clear that Trump admires Putin as well. What other dictators and megalomaniacs does Wild Bill Hiccup admire?

Here's some of what is known about Andrew "Bloody" Jackson, the real historical figure—the seventh president of these United States. Indian Country listed Andrew Jackson among the worst of U.S. presidents, and he is nicknamed "Indian Killer" and "Sharp Knife." Jackson practiced brutal campaigns of genocide against Native people and while in office signed into law the Indian Removal Act—which legalized ethnic cleansing and allowed the forced removal of the Cherokee, Chickasaw, Choctaw, Creek, and Seminole from their homelands, to be relocated farther west in a campaign known as the Trail of Tears. In a presidential address Jackson spoke of how true philanthropy allows for the extinction of one generation to make room for another. But he did not mean any random generation; he meant for generations of white settlers, at the expense of Indian lives.

We've all heard "how the West was won," thanks to spaghetti westerns and John Wayne epics, but "how the East was won" isn't an adage seared into the American consciousness. Yet this is what the Trail of Tears, the Indian Removal Act, and Andrew Jackson essentially are: how the East was won. Andrew Jackson, the face of our twenty-dollar bill, is the eastern version of General George Armstrong Custer. The wild west began in the White House's proverbial wild West Wing.

On the same day, January 24, 2017, when Trump was looking over the White House art collection and deciding to hang the portrait of what many Native Americans equate as Osama bin Laden, in the Oval Office, he also signed off to go ahead with the Dakota Access Pipeline and the Keystone XL pipeline, even though tribal leaders and attorneys have stated time and time again that the pipeline infringes upon treaty rights and threatens to poison the water source for the tribe as well as seventeen million other Americans in close proximity. The Indigenous Environmental Network stated that "these actions by President Trump are insane and extreme, and nothing short of attacks on our ancestral homelands as Indigenous peoples."

And if valorizing Andrew Jackson and signing pipeline orders *on the same day* isn't enough evidence to prove that the president holds no regard whatsoever for Indigenous people or the law or treaties or the environment, he also flagrantly tossed around racial epithets during a White House meeting with senators in early February. Like some Yosemite Sam with a pair of six-shooters, Trump fired off, "Pocahontas is now the face of your party," referring to Senator Elizabeth Warren. Trump has been calling out Senator Warren's questionable claims to Native ancestry for a long time now; however, in previous instances, he wasn't representing the office of POTUS. His use of racial pejoratives—no matter what the context—targeted at Indigenous people is definitely conduct not becoming an officer and a gentleman. But then we already knew that going in, didn't we?

Give a Chump a Chance

Give a chump a chance. Become a chump guardian. You can make a difference.

By sponsoring a White House cabinet member and becoming a Chump Guardian, you will be supporting the Jane McDoGood Institute's initiatives to conserve humanity, protect citizens around the world, and help facilitate necessary care for orphaned chumps at the Sanctuary for Lost Souls outside of Bridgewater, Virginia.

All Chump Guardians receive a photograph of their sponsored chump, their biography, a Chump Guardian certificate, a plush toy chump and bobblehead desk ornament, and fact sheets about their chumps.

About Chumps:

Chumps are mostly intelligent, social beings and cute as the dickens! Before Dr. McDoGood began her groundbreaking study of chumps, little was known of their ecology and behavior in the wild. Dr. McDoGood is a pioneer in the study of chumps, and by installing herself within their habitats, she learned about their ecology, culture, economics, and unique biodiversity. Did you know that chumps make and use tools?! Did you know that chumps form close family bonds?! I know, right?

Chumps currently available for sponsorship:

Mike Pence: Playful "Mikey" was discovered living out of a wooden crate, deprived of all physical contact, and rescued by advocates working for the Sanctuary for Lost Souls. During his early days at the Sanctuary, he couldn't tolerate being touched, but with a lot of patient attention from our care managers and volunteers, Mikey eventually began opening up. Today he loves bright and shiny gadgets and loves to swing. Sponsor Mikey.

Kellyanne Conway: "Chattermouth" was orphaned as a tiny infant and came of age working in a circus. Chattermouth got her nickname because she loves to hear her own voice, and even though her caretakers have not been able to comprehend her attempts at vocalization, it doesn't stop her from nonstop chattering. It has been necessary at times to gag her because her incessant babbling keeps others awake at night. Sponsor Chattermouth.

Betsy DeVos: Betsy loves to climb! And will play for hours with just a piece of string or a rubber ball. Rescued at two years old by a truck driver who discovered her in a dumpster behind the Piggly Wiggly, Betsy has overcome numerous challenges and today is strong and independent; she spends most of her days in trees, laughing and playing with her friends.

Steven Bannon: "Stevie" endured at least fifteen years in a dark, concrete cell and came very close to starving to death before his rescue. He has struggled socially but finally found his place as head of an anti-Semitic fake news organization. Stevie sometimes has difficulty playing with other chumps but has a special friendship with a three-legged puppy he calls Spike. No one ever challenges him, and all the adults, including alpha male Rex, pretend to love him.

Ryan Zinke: It is believed that "RiRi" was born without a soul. Caretakers at the sanctuary do their best to socialize RiRi, but he has not been agreeable and appears to act purely by his own agenda, without taking others into account. He has undergone analysis by Chump psychologists, who have determined that his issues stem from witnessing poachers attacking his village when he was young. Unfortunately, this trauma has caused him to over-identify with poachers. He is immune to kindness. Sponsor RiRi.

Rick Perry: Little "Ricky" is the only known chump to have been raised by wolves and has struggled to reestablish his identity as a chump. Ricky enjoys playing fetch, chasing cars, and impulsively mounting his support staff. He will occasionally try to assert his dominance, but the other chumps don't consider him threatening enough to take seriously. Sponsor Ricky.

Ars Poetica by Donald J. Trump

Nobody, not even the rain, has such small hands.
—E. E. Cummings

Trust me, I'm a poet.
I have all of the words.
I have the best words.
The most tremendous words.
Bigly. Yuge!
Those other poets are a disaster,
just a disaster.
I'm going to build a wall
around those other poet's
words, because no one
has more respect for words than me.
I love words. I respect words so much.
I love them so much that I would date
my own words if I wasn't already
related to them.
I'm going to make poetry great again.
And I'm just the poet to do that too.
When it comes to words—
they're just so beautiful
I just start kissing them,
and I can do that too;
when you're a poet, they let you do that;

they let you do anything.
I'm on those words like a mystic,
I grab 'em by the muse.
Words are great; they're a beautiful thing.
I have the best ones, though,
because I'm the best.
I'm a winner; words love me.
I'm yuge.

Acknowledgments

Grateful acknowledgments to the editors of the following publications in which these essays and articles first appeared, some of them in different forms.

The Butter: "Ghoul, Interrupted," "Headlines," "Redeeming the English Language (Acquisition) Series."

Indian Country Media Network: "Eight Types of Native Moms," "Feast Smudge Snag," "First World (Story) Problems: Brown Girl Multiple Choice Edition," "Attack of the Fifty-Foot (Lakota) Woman," "Trump Pardons Zombie Apocalypse," "A List of Alternative Identities to Try for Fun and Profit," "Champion Our Native Sisters! (but Only Selectively and under Certain Conditions)," "Conversations with My Lakota Mom," "*Wonder Woman* Hits Theaters, Smashes Patriarchy," "Minnesota Art Gallery to Demolish 'Indian Uprisings' Exhibit after Caucasian Community Protest," "I Have White Bread Privilege," "Red like Me: I Knew Rachel Dolezal Back When She Was Indigenous," "Committee of Barnyard Swine to Determine Fate for Women's Health," "Li-Li-Li-Li-Land, Standing Rock, the Musical!" "There's Something about Andrew Jackson," "You've Got Mail!" "The Wild West (Wing) and Wild Bill Hiccup," "Executive Order Requiring All Americans Take Up Cigarettes by End of 2017," "West Wing World," "Give a Chump a Chance," "Step Right Up, Folks," "Things Pseudo-Native

Authors Have Claimed to Be but Actually Are Not," "Reel Indians Don't Eat Quiche: The Fight for Authentic Roles in Hollywood," "Post-Election U.S. Open in Racist Tirades Competition," "Are You There, Christmas? It's Me, Carol!" "Trump Administration to Repeal Bison as First National Mammal," "Thousands of Jingle Dress Dancers Magically Appear at Standing Rock Protector Site," "Post-Election Message to the 53 Percent," "Thanksgiving Shopping at Costco: I Just Can't Even," "Hey America, I'm Taking Back Thanksgiving," "Politically Correct Alternatives to Culturally Insensitive Halloween Costumes," "Clown Costumes Banned, Racist Native American Halloween Costumes Still Okay," "Ars Poetica by Donald J. Trump."

Lit Hub: "Why I Don't Like 'Pussy Hats.'"

McSweeney's: An Open Letter to White Women Concerning *The Handmaid's Tale* and America's Historical Amnesia," "An Open Letter to White Girls Regarding Pumpkin Spice and Cultural Appropriation."

Moss: "The Jimmy Report."

Okey-Pankey: "My Name Is Moonbeam McSwine."

Quarterly West: "Fertility Rites."

Queen Mob's Teahouse: "You Might Be a Pretendian."

The Raven Chronicles: "The Siam Sequences."

The Rumpus: "Tweets as Assigned Texts for a Native American Studies Course."

Sovereign Bodies: "Fifty Shades of Buckskin" was originally published under the title "Love American (Indian) Style."

Waxwing: "First World (Story) Problems: Brown Girl Multiple Choice Edition."

World Literature Today: "Bury My Heart at Chuck E. Cheese's."

"Redeeming the English Language (Acquisition) Series" and "Fertility Rites," anthologized in *Shapes of Native Nonfiction: Collected Essays by Contemporary Writers*, edited by Elissa Washuta and Theresa Warburton (Seattle: University of Washington Press, 2019).

Special thanks to *Indian Country Today* editors, Vince, Ray, I appreciate the space, thank for cheering me on. Thank you, Geary, for your support and abundance. Thank you to Devon, for your bright humor, intelligence, and friendship. My friend Frankie, your love and support mean the world. To Jackie and Litsa, you righted the waters and picked me up when I fell. Thank you, Ms. Fiona, I love you. Thank you to Julie for keeping me sane. I love you. Thank you, Jay, for all of the many untold hours of laughter. I love you. No one makes me laugh as often or as hard—even your bad jokes are good.

Printed in the USA
CPSIA information can be obtained
at www.ICGtesting.com
LVHW092342301123
765247LV00018B/282/J

9 781496 215574